THE ROAD TO
EMMAUS

THE ROAD TO
EMMAUS

RODOLFO G. IBAÑEZ, PH.D., M.D. (H.C.-MMS)

THE ROAD TO EMMAUS

RODOLFO G. IBAÑEZ, PH.D., M.D. (H.C.-MMS)

Published in 2010 by

ST PAULS
7708 St. Paul Road, San Antonio Village
1203 Makati City, Philippines
Tel. (632) 8959701 to 04 • (632) 8966771
Fax. (632) 8907131
Website: www.stpauls.ph
E-mail for orders: wholesale@stpauls.ph

Copyright © 2010
ST PAULS PHILIPPINES
ISBN 978-971-004-085-8 (Hardbound)
ISBN 978-971-004-075-9 (Softbound)
Light Readings and Inspirationals

Printing Information:
Current Printing: first digit

1	2	3	4	5	6	7	8	9	10

Year of current printing: first year shown

2010	2011	2012	2013	2014	2015

ST PAULS is an apostolate of the priests and brothers of the SOCIETY OF ST. PAUL
who proclaim the Gospel through the media of social communication.

TABLE OF CONTENTS

MESSAGE

Christ the King Parish
Greenmeadows Ave., Quezon City
Tel. No. 633-0280

With great pleasure I acceded to the request of Dr. Rodolfo Ibañez to write a short introduction. Actually a twofold pleasure. Firstly, because Rudy is a good friend; secondly, because the Gospel story of the two disciples on the road to Emmaus is one of my favorite Lucan passages.

I have known the author as one of the special ministers of Communion in the Parish of Christ the King—quiet, unassuming, even self-affacing. I did not know until only recently about his accomplishments and the string of national recognition given him for those achievements.

His daily participation in the celebration of the mass and his commitment to his duty as Eucharistic Minister has always edified me. I believe it is this spirituality that underpinned his rereading of, and reflection on, St. Luke's story. His imaginative re-creation of the story makes its timeless message impact on contemporary lives.

My warmest congratulations to Dr. Rudy with my blessing and prayers for more heartwarming and inspiring work.

+ RAUL Q. MARTINEZ, DD
Bishop Emeritus of Antique
March 15, 2010

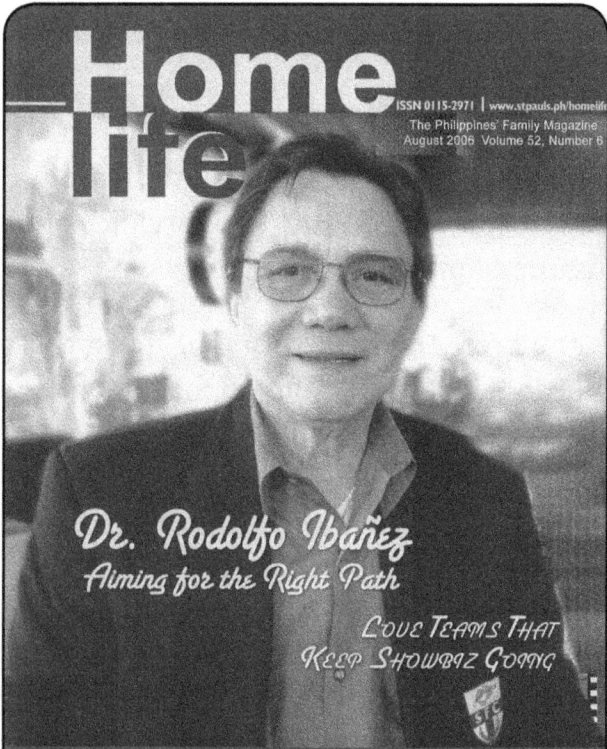

Home life

ISSN 0115-2971 | www.stpauls.ph/homelife
The Philippines' Family Magazine
August 2006 Volume 52, Number 6

Dr. Rodolfo Ibañez
Aiming for the Right Path

LOVE TEAMS THAT
KEEP SHOWBIZ GOING

**Let Us Understand
the Word "Sin"**

• **I Got Pregnant by a Married Man**
• **GOD IS LOVE**
  Pope Benedict XVI's First Encyclical
• **Turning Vegetarian**

AUTHOR'S NOTE

Thinking Pinoy is a column in *HomeLife* magazine, ST PAULS Publication that I write for. The gracious editorial staff even considered some of my articles as cover material and it is my honor to have received such recognition.

HomeLife magazine has been in existence for more than 50 years. The publishers feel that the magazine has already served its purpose in its present style. It may soon come up with an entirely new approach to reach its readers so please watch out for it.

A friend, who also writes for the magazine, suggested that I publish these pieces of wisdom that I have written for the young and the not-so-young into a compilation. But doing so might not lead to enough impact as I would hope for. The true value of my writing is in the way the lessons can be weaved into one unifying story to sweep you into, hopefully, an enlightened experience. And it is my wish that I have succeeded as you enjoy reading what you have in your hands right now.

I included one or two stories that have found print in my other works praying that the message of Jesus Christ Resurrection, forgiveness, is clearly understood.

While the faces you see in the book are real people, I have masked their names in gratitude for letting me share our stories with you.

RGI
Manila, Philippines
March 10, 2010

ACKNOWLEDGMENT

*I*n writing *The Road to Emmaus*, I received invaluable help from my high school friend, Mr. Ruben Evangelista Reyes. Ben's deep research added authenticity to the historical background of the book. The well-written anecdotes accompanying the research truly enriched the book immensely.

I have also published four books in the recent past and all made into easy reading by the editing of my "daughter," Ms. Bunny Ty. She helped make *Memories To Remember, The Class of '55* win the prestigious 2008 Jaime Cardinal Sin Best Book Award during the Catholic Mass Media Awards. She outdid herself in this book.

My wife, Leth, and my two daughters, Leah and Nikki, held my hand as I wrote this book. They kept me going and I am grateful for that. For always.

This is our chapel in the farm, the one my wife built.
Happy faces adorn the chapel because they are part of
the celebration of the Holy Eucharist.

Now, imagine yourself in the time of the Resurrection and in the fashion
of the time, long clothes covering the body of both men and women, long
hairs even for men who are all bearded. You have traveled as a group
and transported yourselves in a place called Emmaus to hear the Teacher
speak in the synagogue, our chapel of today. A great surprise is coming
your way.

And so our story begins…

PROLOGUE

$\mathcal{I}$ was in deep thought.

But Fr. Joe, my spiritual director, was still his usual self. He continued to animatedly explain life lessons to me that only a man of his saintly character can come up with. It is Tuesday morning and I sit here chatting with him just as I always have as far back as I can remember.

This man changed my life.

Before I met him, I recall that I would tell myself, as long as I go to Mass on Sundays, I have fulfilled my obligations to the Lord. As long as I do not miss my confession during Lent and my yearly communion, I should be okay.

My weekly chat with Fr. Joe changed all that. Through him, I learned more about what my Catholic faith means to me. And he has taught me that I can be a saint, right now, right here in the middle of the world. According to him, I need not be a religious that belongs to an order or likewise be like him, an ordained priest. Apparently, Saint Jose Maria has changed the rules. Because of him, the Vatican has become more open to exploring the teachings of Christ in the ordinariness of our lives. This means a lot to true believers and followers of Christ like me. During this particular Tuesday, Fr. Joe told me the story of the Resurrection in the hope that I appreciate what death means even more. He also explained why the Resurrection is the core of Christ's teaching and opened his Bible to the page of the beautiful encounter with two of his disciples on the road to Emmaus.

> *Now that very day [the first day of the week] two of them were going to a village seven miles from Jerusalem called Emmaus, and they were conversing about all the things that had occurred. And it happened that while they were conversing and debating, Jesus himself drew near and walked with them, but their eyes were prevented from recognizing him. He asked them, "What are you discussing as you walk along?" They stopped, looking downcast.*
>
> *One of them, named Cleopas, said to him in reply, "Are you the only visitor to Jerusalem who does not know of the things that have taken place there in these days?"*
>
> *And he replied to them, "What sort of things?"*
>
> *They said to him, "The things that happened to Jesus the Nazarene, who was a prophet mighty in deed and word before God and all the people, how our chief priests and rulers both handed him over to a sentence of death and crucified him. But we were hoping that he would be the one to*

redeem Israel; and besides all this, it is now the third day since this took place. Some women from our group, however, have astounded us: they were at the tomb early in the morning and did not find his body; they came back and reported that they had indeed seen a vision of angels who announced that he was alive. Then some of those with us went to the tomb and found things just as the women had described, but him they did not see."

And he said to them, "Oh, how foolish you are! How slow of heart to believe all that the prophets spoke! Was it not necessary that the Messiah should suffer these things and enter into his glory?"

Then beginning with Moses and all the prophets, he interpreted to them what referred to him in all the scriptures. As they approached the village to which they were going, he gave the impression that he was going on farther. But they urged him, "Stay with us, for it is nearly evening and the day is almost over." So he went in to stay with them.

And it happened that, while he was with them at table, he took bread, said the blessing, broke it, and gave it to them. With that their eyes were opened and they recognized him, but he vanished from their sight. Then they said to each other, "Were not our hearts burning [with us] while he spoke to us on the way and opened the scriptures to us?" (Luke 24:13-32).

To the people of Jerusalem then, the event of that week was big. It did not escape notice from anyone. It was the most talked about happening in the city and its neighboring countryside. It was no wonder that the disciple was surprised to hear the question of Jesus.

For most of us, we remember where we are and what we were doing when major national events happen. I was much younger when the assassination of President Kennedy happened. But I remember it vividly like it was yesterday, how it captivated the whole world and for months, people kept close on the headlines of every newspaper, television studio, and radio network. It was hard not to be involved because in its own way, it affected our personal lives somehow.

The Kennedy assassination was that one single event that pushed the Americans deeper into the Vietnam war because the hawks in Congress, led by the new President Lyndon Johnson, had pushed the young men and women to an unjust war. This prompted the erasure of the myth that U.S. might is indestructible. The poor Vietnamese, fighting only in their black pajama-looking ensemble, humbled the superpower of the world into submission.

I am guessing that it happened the same way in Emmaus. The death and resurrection of the Lord signaled the beginning of the fall of the most powerful army of the ancient times, the Romans. This event paved the way for the blossoming of the new Christian world.

Of course, its impact takes on a different meaning for every person, race, and creed. For me, hearing Fr. Joe tell the story of

Emmaus kept me awake in the next few days. I wanted to know more about it and what it may personally mean to me and hopefully, to you. I craved for more details and background.

And as the days passed, I encountered many written works about this particular event in the road to Emmaus. I found out that numerous books and journals have been published about it and even renowned speakers refer to it. Yet none of what I read captures enough the powerful dialogue that took place between them.

It is my hope that this book gleans on the lessons the disciples learned on their way to Emmaus from the Man who came unannounced and unknown.

As a writer, I can only dream of witnessing and hearing the exchange of words that took place during that time. And as a faithful follower, I can only yearn to be part of that group that walked towards Emmaus. What did they talk about? What could have I heard? Could it have changed who I am today?

This is what I attempt to write.

PREFACE

$\mathcal{I}$t could have been a simple, ordinary request from a long-time friend were it not for its awesome hoped-for object!

When he wrote two of his earlier four books, I somehow got involved helping with a few lines of researched materials.

Hearing from my friend, a fellow alumnus of Class 1955 of Arellano (Public) High School, was most welcomed.

The excitement in his voice was palpable when he declared, "*Pare*, I am writing my fifth book. Please help me with a few lines. They will be among the highlights of my new book."

Without any hesitation, prodded by an instant recollection of how easily I was able to obtain his previously requested materials, I readily assented.

Before he answered my question about what his requested "lines" might be, he ran through a brief description of his new book which he titled *The Road to Emmaus*.

Then he continued, "…can you please help me with the data from your sources to enable me to complete the book's section, "How Did Jesus Christ Look Like?"

(Did I detect a small degree of hesitancy with his spiel when asked me that?)

With my 20/20 vision hindsight, I realized I should not have been too quick saying yes to my present "assignment." Why, I do not even know how my paternal grandparents looked like!

Even the pinhole camera the ancestor of the present-day digital camera was still light years away from Jesus' time. The Bible was graphic with the details of his wounds, bruises, and welts as a result of the heavy scourging he received. But aside from his piercing eyes, nothing else was written about how exactly he looked like. In terms of popularity, or notoriety, however mundane and shallow, Pilate and a handful of Roman officials assured theirs when their respective profiles were struck on coins.

But, of course, not Jesus who was considered by the state as enemy number one in his time.

A few weeks later, I was able to draw from a number of books by religious writers, from paintings and other artworks by the masters, even from the controversial Shroud of Turin, and, of course, from Wikipedia.

The description I eventually sent to my friend, a composite actually, of how Jesus might have looked liked, was the best

I could do. Never mind how feeble and too far-fetched they may be from the actual physical features of Jesus.

But what about those masters and illustrious religious authors whose works are presently used by researches of similar subject? Definitely they faced a much more dearth of reference materials. How then they were able to put on canvas and on paper their impressive renderings of Jesus' image?

The French novelist, Antoine de Saint-Exupery, provided the answer. In his famous book, there was this conversation between the pilot and the Little Prince:

> "The men where you live," said the Little Prince, "raise five thousand roses in the same garden— and they do not find in it what they are looking for."
> "They do not find it," I replied.
> "And yet what they are looking for could be found in a single rose or in a little water."
> "Yes, that is true," I said.
> And the Little Prince added: "But the eyes are blind. One must look with the heart…"

The masters and the authors undoubtedly looked with their own hearts.

Similarly, my friend, Dr. Rodolfo G. Ibañez, has once again written from his heart for his latest book *The Road to Emmaus*.

The risen Christ first appeared before Mary Magdalene. Later, the second of his eleven recorded appearances.

He revealed himself to the two common travelers to Emmaus, a small village not far from Jerusalem.

As one reads through *The Road to Emmaus*, it soon becomes apparent to the reader why Dr. Ibañez decided on that title.

Life is a journey. Over time, we have our own Roads to traverse—through happiness and despair, pleasure and pain, peace and conflict, success and failures.

Inevitably, there are times when we find our road jaggedly rocky or slippery with mud. There will be the twists and turns and bends and the problematic forks. We are confronted with all sorts of obstacles which make our forward trek painfully slow. Then at the end of our road we may be staggered by a sheer precipice. Only the crags and sharp abutments of a rocky cliff are available for the perilous trudge downhill towards our destination. The darkening skies laden with ominous storm clouds do not improve our situation.

Indeed, against this scenario we become helpless and hopeless. We feel lost. We meet the moment of defeat. We are convinced and lament we are traveling alone. We pathetically acknowledge we cannot hazard another step without help from someone greater than ourselves.

At this precise moment, we look heavenward and turn over our difficulties and aggravations to God. We realize we must surrender our situation to him, completely. Often we are reminded that he has the perfect blueprint for our lives.

Then his miraculous work begins.

We come upon a joyous discovery which is extremely reassuring.

In Matthew 28:20, Jesus gave his assurance: *"And behold, I am with you always, until the end of the age."*

With him by our side, we will never walk alone.

This is the central theme of *The Road to Emmaus*, the fifth book heart-written by Dr. Rodolfo G. Ibañez.

RUBEN EVANGELISTA REYES
Arellano High School
Class of '55

RESURRECTION

The Cornerstone of Christian Faith

*E*mmaus, meaning, warm spring. An ancient town located approximately seven miles northwest of present-day Jerusalem. According to Christian scripture, Jesus appeared before two of his followers in Emmaus after his resurrection.

Now that very day [the first day of the week] two of them were going to a village seven miles from Jerusalem called Emmaus, and they were conversing about all the things that had occurred. And it happened that while they were conversing and debating, Jesus himself drew near and walked with them, but their eyes were prevented from recognizing him. He asked them, "What are you discussing as you walk along?" They stopped, looking downcast.

One of them, named Cleopas, said to him in reply, "Are you the only visitor to Jerusalem who does not know of the things that have taken place there in these days?"

And he replied to them, "What sort of things?"

They said to him, "The things that happened to Jesus the Nazarene, who was a prophet mighty in deed and word before God and all the people, how our chief priests and rulers both handed him over to a sentence of death and crucified him. But we were hoping that he would be the one to redeem Israel; and besides all this, it is now the third day since this took place. Some women from our group, however, have astounded us: they were at the tomb early in the morning and did not find his body; they came back and reported that they had indeed seen a vision of angels who announced that he was alive.

Then some of those with us went to the tomb and found things just as the women had described, but him they did not see." And he said to them, "Oh, how foolish you are! How slow of heart to believe all that the prophets spoke! Was it not necessary that the Messiah should suffer these things and enter into his glory?" Then beginning with Moses and all the prophets, he interpreted to them what referred to him in all the scriptures.

As they approached the village to which they were going, he gave the impression that he was going on farther. But they urged him, "Stay with us, for it is nearly evening and the day is almost over." So he went in to stay with them.

And it happened that, while he was with them at table, he took bread, said the blessing, broke it, and gave it to them. With that their eyes were opened and they recognized him, but he vanished from their sight. Then they said to each other, "Were not our hearts burning [with us] while he spoke to us on the way and opened the scriptures to us?"

So they set out at once and returned to Jerusalem where they found gathered together the eleven and those with them who were saying, "The Lord has truly been raised and has appeared to Simon!" Then the two recounted what had taken place on the way and how he was made known to them in the breaking of the bread.

—Luke 24:13-35

CHAPTER I

I Dream of Emmaus

David and John—The Dreamers

I am David the man from the present who had a dream and that dream became real with the help of my friend, John. We are both dreamers. Continue to imagine yourself in the time of the Resurrection. Read on...

$\mathcal{T}$he Program Committee was busy planning the 55th Anniversary of the Arellano High School Class '55. Yes, you read right. We marched out of our beloved school's main gate for the last time as students 55 years ago and the year was 1955.

Our planning session did not take long. We were inspired by the success of our Golden Jubilee five years ago and this coming anniversary is going to be a mere takeoff from that. Septuagenarians as we are, we spent more time talking about our aching bones and thinning hair!

With a few hours to spare before heading home, I decided to go ahead and walk down memory lane, namely, the streets of Doroteo Jose, Lope de Vega, and Zurbaran.

Doroteo was where the pinball and football arcade machines were located. It was the TimeZone and Power Station of today. This was the entertainment capital of the Arellanites. We shared it together with the more affluent Mapua Tech students. These pinball machines afforded us a few minutes of fun during the day—all for a five-centavo coin. I played these machines numerous times and can even remember every bit of the dings, bangs, and clicks of the machines until today.

Moving further down Doroteo Jose, I was pleasantly surprised to still see the bookstore that I frequented over fifty years ago! The owner's children now operate the store that sells only previously-owned books. This has always been my favorite bookstore because I like the way the owners thoughtfully arranges their books by genre.

Like it's always been even as a student, I was drawn to the Inspirational and Religious Books section. And what do you know; there staring right back at me was a copy of the book I've been looking for! Written in 1949, *The Greatest Story Ever Told* by Fulton Oursler has long gone out of print. It retells the story of Jesus Christ in a novel-like fashion. It is a sequel to *The Greatest Story Ever Told* which tells the story of the Old Testament. The third in the series is called *The Greatest Faith Ever Known* which tells the story of Peter, Paul, and the other Apostles. Unfortunately, the author passed away before finishing the book and it was his daughter, April, who had to complete this particular piece.

Very gingerly, I took the book from the shelf and sat on a chair by the corner. Leafing through the pages, I was captivated.

"David! Hello, David!"

I was startled by this unexpected greeting. Could it be someone from work? Almost all my family and friends call me Dave except for my *Nanay* who would scream, "DAVIIIIIID!!!" at the top of her lungs whenever she saw me reaching for the family's ancient vase when I was a little boy.

I looked up and saw a bearded face smiling at me. He had a full set of white sparking teeth, his beard and eyebrows were thick and gray, neatly trimmed and stood out in contrast to his bald shiny head. He also had piercing blue eyes and looked to me like he was Middle-Eastern.

"Do I know you?" I asked.

He extended his hand and smiled again. "I am Cleopas, that's without an H."

"What do I care if your name has an H or not. I don't know you," I mused.

"It matters," he said. "Cleopas with an H was the husband of Mary who was one of the women in Israel who stayed around the Cross."

"Now, he's going biblical," I thought to myself.

"Aaah, that's good. You remember the Bible!"

I nearly fell off my chair. He can read my mind!

"I was one of the two disciples that traveled together with Jesus to Emmaus."

I looked at him with wary eyes. Either I was hallucinating or this man was a lunatic. Not meaning to be rude, I listened to what he had to say.

"It was in the afternoon of what you now know as Easter Sunday. There have been rumors going around the locals that the crucified Christ was raised from his grave."

I've read the Bible so I know what he was talking about. Now he'll tell me about Mary Magdalene, I thought to myself.

"Apparently," the man kept going, "it was Mary of Magdala who saw him first. Or perhaps more accurately, he made himself seen as she went on her way to visit his tomb. My companion and I had to rush to Emmaus for an important meeting with the other disciples. We simply wanted to hear it from Peter himself to believe it."

"If you really are one of the disciples as you claim to be, why did you need to get Peter's confirmation? Were you not present during those times that Jesus foretold his death, and resurrection on Easter Sunday? Or did you simply not believe him?" I asked testily.

He acted like he didn't hear a word that I said. Cleopas went on to tell me that halfway through Emmaus, a stranger had asked permission if he could walk with them. He then claimed to feel a sudden and inexplicable sense of peace in the presence of this stranger. He said it could just have been his imagination but suddenly, the trees around them looked greener, the birds sang louder, and the flowers smelled sweeter. He looked around if anyone else had noticed and his companions all looked like their hearts were burning with some mysterious fervor.

The stranger then asked, "What is all this commotion about? Why is everyone so eager and in awe of someone or something appearing?"

Cleopas then admitted to me, "I couldn't help but be sarcastic. I had to ask the stranger where he had been this whole week. It's like he has been living under a rock! But I just went ahead and explained to him about the capture of Jesus in the garden when one of the disciples tipped the authorities of his identity and whereabouts. I went on to tell him about the mock trial, the gruesome scene at Mount Golgotha, the sudden darkness in the skies, the fearsome earthquake, and how it all happened one right after the other. Three people were executed by crucifixion, the most painful and cruel retribution of all, two thieves and Jesus, the Rabbi. Then the following Sunday morning, there was incredible news that Jesus, who always claimed to be the Son of God, and who died and was buried in a donated tomb, has risen. Imagine that! He had reportedly come back from the dead!"

I couldn't help but notice his tentativeness, "Reportedly? Why do you doubt your recount of such an awe-inspiring experience? Perhaps you and your companions mistakenly took the news halfheartedly and did not fully believe in Jesus when he declared that he will rise from his tomb on the third day. Surely you were there when Jesus returned Lazarus and that little girl to life. Were you there?"

I think I offended Cleopas who looked away from me when he said, "I know. We should have had enough faith in him and believed without question the promises he made. But can you blame us? We were limited men, quite short in logic. We figured, how can he resurrect himself from his deathbed? How can that even be possible? It was too profound a realization for us to even consider then. But now we are more aware that God never asked us to understand; we only need to trust his pronouncements. He had said, "My thoughts are not your thoughts.""

There was a moment of silence between us. Cleopas reached into his trouser pockets and took out a soft leather bag. He offered me its contents, dates? Is this for real? They were fresh ones. Something I have never seen before except for the packed ones sold in supermarkets.

And although dates in particular are not mentioned in the Bible, the tree from where it came from has been written about. My encounter with Cleopas was beginning to intrigue me. I took a couple and they tasted sweet and fleshy with a tinge of sourness. I slipped the seeds into my pocket as we continued to chat.

Cleopas continued, "You remember the stranger I told you about? He also picked up on my disbelief just as you did. He said it was a sign of spiritual weakness. And then he scolded me on the significance and the true meaning of the prophecies concerning the Messiah. I admit, I found his insight and knowledge marvelous. Quite unusual perhaps, but still entertaining at least for the rest of our walk. It was getting dark so I went ahead and invited him to spend the night with us. He agreed."

"As we sat down for supper, the stranger took the bread, pronounced the blessing, broke it, and began to distribute it to us. I immediately recognized the ritual. It was exactly like our Last Supper three days ago. I could not believe that I had not recognized him. None of us did. I guess, our hearts have truly hardened."

With that their eyes were opened and they recognized him, but he vanished from their sight (Luke 24:31).

Then it was my turn to be quiet. My heart was racing. If this man is authentic, then I am with someone who has been face-to-face with Jesus himself!

I could not believe it.

So I ventured and asked, "What did Jesus look like? Does he look the same as what we have believed him to look like?"

Cleopas apologized and did not give me a straight answer. All he said was that, "The Child grew and became strong; he was full of wisdom and God's blessings were upon him."

I have read that before in the gospel of Luke. His response, just like in the Bible and in the New Testament, was philosophical.

And then he went on, "During our relentless trek on the roads and hills of Galilee, Jesus filled his hours with sermons and recitations of parables. His eyes always flamed with prophetic visions. And always, there would be an immense crowd of listeners who were visibly awestruck by his eloquence. Nobody has ever talked the way this man does!"

Some writers have said that Jesus had a golden voice. He possessed an extraordinary skill at dialectics. Cleopas agrees with me, "We, as his disciples, are not exempt from being captivated by his personal magnetism. We were still in awe each time he gave his discourses. We absorbed every word he uttered like they were precious pearls coming out of his mouth. So much so that I cannot recall what he looked like except for his eyes. But who knows, by chance, you may have the opportunity to meet the Man yourself. The Teacher will, no doubt, fill you with what you are asking me. Bye for now."

And then before I knew it, Cleopas was gone.

I felt a bit disappointed. Here was an actual Emmaus traveler and yet, he would not tell me what Jesus looked like. But then again, he himself did not recognize the resurrected Christ himself and he was already in their midst!

Isn't it ironic how the greatest character in all of history did not leave humanity with a visual reminder of how he looks like? It's just too bad for us then that we have to solely rely on the works of ancient artists and sculptors for a glimpse of the Master's countenance. But in the absence of an actual subject, it is now up to the artist's skills and imagination to create an image strong enough to summon faith and devotion from people who require a visual image of the gods they worship.

However, authors of the Bible believe that the artists who drew Christ were divinely guided and inspired by the

Master himself. This and together with their unwavering determination to gather information from monasteries and convents, reading from the works of ancient writers, and from artifacts that archaeologists have found, anything meant something as long as a mere profile can be created that was true to Christ's likeness.

These are the physical features that they have collected to compose a collage of Christ:

> *Hair:* Long, had not been cut since childhood. (The Jewish youth of biblical times loved to wear their hair long and curled.) Dark brown, curly, not very thick. Shiny and parted in the middle like the Nazarene fashion that time. Flowing over the shoulders and the color of ripe filbert.
>
> *Eyes:* Immense, piercing, and flashing dark eyes. Beautiful, sea-blue and shading into brown with brows that grew together.
>
> *Nose:* Prominent, perfect, and exactly formed.
>
> *Mouth:* Perfect and exactly formed.
>
> *Beard:* Similar to hair color but thicker. Not long but forked.
>
> *Complexion:* Face without blemish or wrinkles. Beautifully oval, comely, olive, and somewhat ruddy.

Height: About 5'11", well-proportioned, look of good health, has a handsome figure, pale but muscular. Exudes perfect tranquility.

Based on these findings, master artists the likes of Michelangelo, Da Vinci, and Raphael went ahead and rendered a canvas of the image of Christ. It was certainly not easy. It took a lengthy period of working under full sunlight or against the flickering of a gaslight until they were satisfied that they have successfully captured the real essence of Christ. It has always been said that God always reveals himself as a presence. Without a doubt, these master artists must have been endowed by the Creator with more than just a gift of artful hands. Surely, they have been gifted with an eerie sensitivity and consciousness to sense his presence and work with it. We will always be indebted to them. Their priceless masterpieces, Da Vinci's *Last Supper*, Francesca's *Baptism of Christ*, Raphael's *Madonna and Child*, Giotto's *Pieta*, and Michelangelo's *Moses* to name a few, have given us something tangible to look at for our faith and devotion to deepen.

There is another artifact reputed to describe the physical Jesus Christ, not in his most joyous moment but in his passion and eventual death. This Shroud of Turin may very well verify his resurrection, the very cornerstone of the Christian faith.

Since the 14th century, an official document has long challenged the authenticity of the Shroud. Experts have yet to resolve three areas concerning the relic. Is it medieval forgery? An occult phenomenon? Or a real proof of the resurrection of Christ?

There has been a wide pendulum of opinions regarding the genuineness of the Shroud since it was discovered more than 400 years ago in Europe. The experts are made up of one Nobel Prize-winning organic and nuclear scientist, prominent pathologists from all over the world, several authorities on carbon dating, reputable radiologists and photographers, biblical scholars, and high personages from the Church hierarchy. Yet they all have not come to a unanimous agreement.

At least, avid anti-Shroud individuals admit to one mystery surrounding the relic: How did the image of a man, plainly crucified, be fully rendered on it?

Dr. Leslie D. Weatherhead, Ph.D., D.D. wrote the most stirring account about Jesus' grave clothes. He is convinced that the fourth Gospel was written based on the account of an actual witness.

> "It is made clear that the grave clothes, covering the body up to the armpits, had collapsed as if the body had evaporated. We are also told that the turban wrapped around his head stood on its edge as if the head had also evaporated."

The first 20 verses in the 20th chapter of the fourth Gospel will show that it was the way the grave clothes laid on the ground that convinced Peter and John that Christ had disposed of his physical body in a way none of us can ever fully comprehend. There was no trace of myrrh and aloe that would suggest that the corpse of Christ has even moved. The grave clothes were still intact, nothing out of place, just that the head and body were now gone. Possibly, evaporation, evanescence, or dematerialization but despite these, still the heart can never completely grasp without faith.

On the other hand, both believers and skeptics have come to agree on how the Shroud looked. Both of them accept the existence of a distinct impression of a human body suggesting that the cloth has been used to wrap a cadaver from head to toe. The hair appear coarse and stringy, probably blood-soaked. It hung almost down to the neck. Blood stains were everywhere including lacerations all over the body which indicates repeated flogging using sharp-tipped thongs. There were large droplets of blood from the hairline which suggests entrance points of a thorn-like material. It was the large gash on the side of his body that showed the most bleeding.

Calculations based on the image of the limbs in the Shroud showed forearms almost 14 inches long which is consistent with a 5'11" body. The same expert who made these findings deduce that the man, who could be Christ himself, was whipped after he was tied while bent over touching his toes. Experts count at least 98 lashes and 125 welts on the body. Trauma marks on the shoulders show that a rough, heavy beam was carried.

Robert K. Wilcox, a well-traveled investigative journalist in search for the truth about the Shroud said, "As mysterious as the shroud was, the face it displayed was remarkably similar to the traditional Christ-type seen on many ancient icons and the religious paintings of early Eastern Christianity. The first depictions of Christ were highly idealized; he was shown as clean-shaven and youthful. Around the sixth century, his image changed. He was now a grown man with long hair, beard, and eyes that were curiously large and ovate. This was the same image on the Shroud."

The controversy of the Shroud has spanned decades and is far from being settled even until today. The question that everyone wants an answer to is this: Is that the same Shroud that Christ used when he resurrected? Because if it is, then, no doubt, the image on the Shroud is that of Christ himself. There will be no more need for scientists to prove how the image on the garment came to be. Because as Reverend Billy Graham so aptly puts it, "Only love can see God. It is not that the Eternal Existence of God is contrary to reason. Rather, it is beyond reason."

"You know what, Christ can look like whatever you want him to look." It was Cleopas who interrupted my thoughts. "He can be your father, your older brother, or your younger siblings, heck, he can even be your great-grandfather if you want. Take the best of these people and even more. Now that should approximate who Christ is and what he looks like."

I know what he meant but it wasn't the answer I was looking for. I was determined to squeeze answers out of him when I felt a nudge on my shoulder.

"Sir? Sir! Wake up!"

"Huh? What time is it?"

"It's a little after three. I think you fell asleep reading that book."

I looked at my watch and realized that I've been sitting in this corner for ten minutes. I must have dozed off and was even dreaming. It must be from the heat and exhaustion.

I thanked the lady and went ahead and bought the book. As I reach for my wallet, I felt something in my pocket.

There were three date seeds.

CHAPTER II

Created in the Image of the Man from Emmaus

In our story, I wrote of Ate Anna,
my sister who is also a mother to all of us.

$\mathcal{M}$y dream of Cleopas never ended even as I woke up. In fact, I could not wait to get back to it once I got home. I took my dream to be a sign, like an invitation from Christ himself to meet him. I have always believed it was him with the way Cleopas said he broke bread.

But Cleopas remained adamant. He insists that during that time, he and the rest of the disciples only thought of him to be the stranger who joined their walk to Emmaus. They had no idea who they were keeping company with.

But I knew. And my heart rejoiced at the possibility of meeting him and relishing in his wisdom. The opportunity to be enlightened was something I have been praying for. To hear my Champion speak of life and love and everything in between overwhelmed me. I have not really thought of what I would say to him but I knew it would start with a thank you, for being in my dreams and in my heart. And because of him, I am not afraid of anything. I welcome life and death, and believe that in my most difficult moments, I shall be lifted and carried. I was beside myself in joy just at that mere thought…

"Are you headed to Emmaus?"

I looked up and was at a loss for words. Here he was already. I managed to fumble a yes. "I have been walking all day since yesterday. I am lonely and I thought I was lost. I saw you from a distance and wondered if I can come along, that is if you are heading there, too," I explained.

"David should be okay," Cleopas assured the Man. "An added person in our group could be of help. Along this road, there will sometimes be brigands who may want to take advantage of us. David can be of help in warding them off just in case. Let's bring him along."

The Man thought for a second and said, "Sure. Come along. And tell us more about yourself."

I wasn't sure where and how to begin. There were so many things I wanted to tell him and so many things I wanted to ask.

"Let me share with you about my *Ate Anna* and hopefully, you'll get to know who I really am."

How I Became Who I Am

You could say that I have always believed I was going to be a champion. I have carried this inspiring thought with me ever since I can remember. That's because my *Ate Anna* said so. And I believe anything she says.

You see, my Ate Anna has been with me ever since I can remember. As a student in the barrio, it was her skirt that I remember holding on to when I stepped into the classroom for the very first time. So my poor *Ate* had no choice but to sit with me through my entire first day of school. "*Ate*, don't leave. *Iiyak po ako pag-iniwan n'yo ako*," I pleaded.

Ate Anna was like a mother to me. The second in our brood of eleven children, she had taken on the responsibility of caring for us while our parents were busy with their jobs. It was she who taught me how to write my name. That was six decades ago. Ate Anna is now living in America like most of my other siblings. She just recently celebrated her 70th birthday and what do you give someone who has done a lot for you? A love letter, of course.

Dear Ate Anna,

The years have been good to us. While it is true that there were times of plenty and times of drought financially and emotionally, don't you think we can say that we are still ahead of life's ups and downs? You have been like a second mother to all of us and, most of all, a friend.

I remember when we were much younger; you would patiently tie the string that held up my pants. You always tied it in your own special way. "Yung may dalawang bilog na buhol, Ate Anna," I always asked you. And before you let me go, you always had me blow my nose on the hem of your skirt because even then, I've always had a problem with my sinuses.

Caring for Nanay in her dying years strained our sibling relationships. Some of us wanted to put her in a senior shelter; some wanted to alternate caring for her. But in your wisdom, you saw the futility of these suggestions. You knew Nanay needed continuous loving care. And as always, you took on that responsibility.

I don't know how you did it but you managed to share the time for your own family to make sure that Tatay's and Nanay's final years will be precious. Kuya Rene has been a very understanding husband. He needed you as much as we did but he was compassionate enough to share you with us because we really needed you.

Today, there is an uneasy peace among us. Sadly, the tension and the harsh words exchanged years ago still continue to create an atmosphere of suspicion and mistrust. It is my hope that we all surpass this and realize that we all need each other. Just think how it will be like when we go back to loving each other as we used to, truly then we have followed Jesus' commandment, "Love one another as I have loved you." And Tatay and Nanay would be smiling at us from above. But alas, I can only ardently pray for that.

Speaking for myself though, let me tell you something that I have read in a book entitled, 365 Days with the Lord. In the book, it says: "Everyone remembers at least one teacher who had influenced his life. These teachers do not just impart knowledge, but a way of life as well. They are worthy of emulation because their wisdom does not come only from books but from life itself. They make an effort to live what they impart to

their students and that in itself is already a very
powerful lesson."

Ate Anna, you are that teacher to me.

"That is very touching, David. And what a way to introduce yourself. It gives us an idea on who you really are through your Ate Anna. I don't know how many people would sacrifice themselves for another. Your Ate Anna is a gem in today's generation," said one of the disciples.

"I remember our own teacher, too," interrupted Cleopas. "He, too, sacrificed himself for us. But what I can't understand is why people still want to hurt him, even kill him. And all he did was cure the sick, help the poor, and show us a better way of life. He died praying to the Father to forgive everyone who may have been involved in his suffering. Even during death, he was thinking of us."

Silence befell our group until broken only by the Teacher, *"These are my words that I spoke to you while I was still with you, that everything written about me in the law of Moses and in the prophets and psalms must be fulfilled. Thus it is written that the Messiah would suffer and rise from the dead on the third day and that repentance, for the forgiveness of sins, would be preached in his name to all the nations, beginning from Jerusalem. You are witnesses of these things. And [behold] I am sending the promise of my Father upon you"* (see Luke 24:44-49).

That got me to think about Ate Anna once again. In her simplicity, she took the message of the Messiah to heart.

She took care of us, more than she took care of herself. Her self-sacrifice made the lives of others better. If only more people did that, the world will certainly be a better place.

Today, my heart is full. Meeting the Messiah in my dreams, I still have another opportunity to wait for his second coming. This gives me a chance to understand his promise of eternity even more. It has inspired me to become a teacher, for he is my guide. And as Christ is with me in my vocation, I am stirred to teach the young and to make a difference just as he did in my life. And now it's time for me to tell him about it.

CHAPTER III
The Teacher of Emmaus

Man of Wisdom!

Many of the lessons shared in this book are from a man of wisdom. In my dream he is the Man that joined Cleopas and the other disciple on the road to Emmaus. We are so lucky to travel with him and listen to his words.

$\mathcal{J}$t is my birthday and I am celebrating Mass with my wife. The bishop had asked us to stay a bit longer after the services to tell us about an e-mail he recently received. And there I was given a wonderful gift by way of a story.

It happened in Egypt.

A Muslim man killed his wife because she was reading the Bible. He was so angry that he buried his daughters alive with their dead mother. To seek revenge, he reported it to the police and wrongfully accused another family member of the crime.

Fifteen days later, another family member died and was buried. It was then that they found the two girls buried under the sand. They were alive!

The country became outraged because of what happened and the man was scheduled to be executed at the end of the month.

When the eight-year-old girl was asked how she survived, she said, "A man wearing shiny white clothes with bleeding wounds in his hands came to feed us every day. And he woke my Mom up so she could nurse my sister."

A veiled Muslim woman anchor was interviewing her on national TV when the girl added, "The man was none other than Jesus because nobody else does things like these."

The Muslims weren't surprised. After all, they believe that *Isa* (Jesus) was capable of doing this. And the bleeding wounds only meant one thing—that he was crucified. Yet... he was still alive. Everyone believed the little girl because that was the only way she could have survived being buried alive for 15 days. Only a miracle could make that happen.

After hearing the little girl's account of the story, Muslim leaders had a difficult time reconciling the events. And with Egypt being the center of media and education in the Middle East, the amazing story spread like wildfire. Indeed, Christ still presides over us and the world. He has his ways.

For days, I could not shake the story off. I could not stop thinking about the little girls, the miracle that happened, and what it meant to me even if I was halfway across the world. I also wondered about the Muslims in the Middle East especially those who were witnesses to the story. Ultimately, they are our brothers as much as Christians, Hindus, and even as much as the followers of Asian mystics are. I wondered how they were taking the news.

Like the teachers of Emmaus, my bishop is guided by the Holy Spirit in reminding me about the teachings of Christ. As a teacher myself, I could only wish that I can be as inspiring to my students as well. This is every bit of a challenge in spite of having been in the academe in the last ten years and in the workforce in the last 35! I find teaching a course on human behavior quite grueling. You know how it is; people are such a sensitive topic. It is almost impossible to be dogmatic especially when it comes to human sensibilities.

I was barely three years into teaching when I was offered the honor of running an entire university. I was to spearhead a new program in the country–transnational education. And as head of the school, I was an influential player in this university's future. What a great honor it was and an even greater opportunity to implement my vision of what a true learning environment should be.

Nurturing Environment

When I was going to school, I remember how teachers and students were pitted against each other. Like they were meant to be on separate teams and one group's success had to be to the detriment of the other. I want to change that. It wasn't going to happen especially in my university.

When asked of my plan, I explained, "Our prime responsibility is to our students and faculty, to go beyond their expectations of learning and achievement. That is the core of this university's mission statement. It will project the powerful image of what we are about and the kind of daily existence that we permeate in the world."

I then recalled what Pope John Paul I wrote about Giosuè Carducci, a professor of Bologna University. Professor Carducci attended a forum in Florence and impressed the Minister of Education so much that he was requested to stay another day.

"I can't, your Excellency," he replied, "I have a lecture at the university tomorrow and my students will be waiting."

"It's all right, I can excuse you," the Minister said.

"You may excuse me, Sir, but I cannot excuse myself. My students will be disappointed," he answered apologetically.

With this reply, the Pope considers Professor Carducci with high regard. He truly had an admirable sense of commitment to both the school and his students. He is the kind of teacher who believes that more than just instruction; teachers must also know and love their students. This is the best environment for learning and growing. If only our sense of commitment to teaching is always this heartening.

I was greatly inspired by Professor Carducci and today, I can proudly say that our university boasts a 26% student population who are in the honor roll. That figure should speak for itself into showing you how collective the efforts of our faculty and staff are in creating such an impact into teaching our students.

Likewise, our students look at our classrooms as an arena for intellectual exercise and moral transformation. There is something explosive that happens within our four walls, great minds clash in search of truth echoing tradition and ideas that may eventually create the blueprint of our future. In the words of Colin Powell, statesman, diplomat, and general, "The challenge is to find the balance between fiction that lowers performance and distinctiveness that lifts performance."

Trust plays a key role in our learning environment. A promise made, a word spoken, and gestures to help are all seen as a bond that seals the deep relationship our teachers share with their students. It asks much from each of them but there is also a willingness to forge a learning relationship like no other.

This is the same relationship Christ had with his students on their walk to Emmaus.

The Bamboo Plant

A momentary silence befell upon the group; *parang may anghel na dumaan* as Filipino elders would say.

A female student, who looked much younger than her 21 years of age and had her hair up, arranged with a simple ponytail, raised her hand politely.

I called on her.

"I just have a question, Sir. I have a frequent boy-visitor at our place. Although I find him interesting, I am not so sure if I can call him a good conversationalist. My Dad is usually around when he visits and he enjoys lecturing him to no end.

My friend enjoys historical trivia and can narrate about the Middle East, Russia, and even about the Spanish Inquisition. He also possesses a knack for useless trivia. He once told my father that the word testimony came from the word testicles because it was customary in ancient Rome that men place their right hand on their testicles when taking an oath. Or how Saint Nicholas, the original Father Christmas, was a patron saint of thieves, virgins, and communist Russia. I actually find him boring but my Dad thinks he is a genius."

"'Yung batang 'yan maituturing kong napaka-edukado! Ang dami n'yang alam!"

The girl sounded frustrated and we all knew why. I knew too well what this girl was feeling. I have met these sorts of characters in my own life and there is nothing more exasperating than being caught in the middle of their discussion! Their information may be head-on but their opinions are usually shallow and simplistic. Such persons may be well-informed but there is no discernment in their thoughts. Insight calls for artistic judgment and astuteness and these are hard to come by when a person is too caught up in his facts and figures.

There was another long pause before I replied, "An educator once wrote that the aim of education or culture is the encouragement and development of good taste in knowledge and good form in conduct. One need not be well-read or learned to be considered ideally educated or cultured. It is definitely more than that. The educated and cultured man is one who likes and dislikes the right things. To know what to love and what to hate is to have taste in knowledge. Your boy-visitor may be a collector and lover of trivia but he is certainly no scholar. It is quite easy to gather and memorize facts; all you need is a good memory. On the other hand, it is quite a task to be able to discern which fact and figure is significant and worth remembering. And having insight on certain things requires a considerable depth of understanding."

"I once asked a friend how come his youngest child was enrolled in a relatively lesser known school. He told me that it was his wife who wanted their child there after reading their school's creed. It said, *We believe that children, even as adults, become that which they live and if we are to achieve such goals, we can do so only to the extent that we set up situations that will make this living possible. To discover this, we constantly speak in terms of each individual child and see what he is as he comes to us and what hopes and dreams he will have for a better tomorrow. He will always live in a social world; therefore, the conditions under which he must learn must be kept primarily social.*

This small school therefore was created to be a place where all these qualities are to be made possible—to develop initiative, responsibility, and self-direction, to be able to think, evaluate objectively, and make decisions in socially-conscious ways. It must be made possible for a child to love these qualities in everyday situations until they become a part of him."

"Remember this," I said, "where we begin determines our destination. A good education is an excellent starting place. President John F. Kennedy at one time admonished, 'Let us think of education as the means of developing our greatest abilities because in each of us, there is a private hope and dream which, when fulfilled, can be translated into being beneficial to everyone and poses as a greater strength for our nation.' "

"Think of the bamboo plant," the Messiah continued my thoughts, "after its seeds are planted, no visible growth takes place for up to five years. Then as if by magic, a sprout appears and then grows at the rate of nearly two and a half feet per day until it reaches its full height of 90 feet within six weeks. But there is no magic. Its rapid growth is due to the unimaginable growth of its root system that develops underground in the first five years. And so it is with the hidden years of educating yourselves!"

Again, there was silence broken only by another student who said, "Teacher, speak to us about change."

I can take a shot at answering that question by way of a story of Anna.

The Story of Anna

Anna closed their front door. It was getting late but she promised to attend Rachel's going-away party. After all, her friend has been offered a scholarship to the only university in the country offering transnational education. Anna was happy for Rachel. Her friend now has the opportunity none of them from their high school will ever have.

It wasn't unexpected. From the very beginning of their friendship, Anna already knew that Rachel had a brilliant mind and there were great things waiting for her. As Anna walked towards Rachel's house, she was surprised when someone stepped in to join her.

"Mom!"

"I know you're headed to Rachel's party and I thought I'd walk along with you."

"Okay," Anna said with a bit of confusion.

"You have been through a lot with Rachel. And now she is leaving for Manila, you can just imagine the drastic change about to happen," her Mom said.

"What is it that you want to talk about," Anna asked directly.

"Rachel's life is changing but so is yours. I care about you and I want you to be ready especially when Rachel leaves. Because I know that for most of your life, Rachel has been the only friend you have had," her Mom said as her voice broke a little.

"I'm not sure what you mean," Anna said now, feeling a bit sensitive and defensive.

"Let me tell you something about life in Manila. It's very different there. People there are more liberal. They will shrug off many of the things we practice and believe here at home. I even heard that students there go to school dressed in house clothes and slippers as if they don't care about what the world thinks of them!"

Her Mom stopped talking for a second, afraid that she might have already made Anna angry and upset. But Anna seemed insulted as well and retorted back, "Mom, I think that will be least of Rachel's problems! We've read about her university in the Internet. She knows what she is getting into. In fact, she knows that some of the students and teachers there are foreigners. And at best, she's more worried about being able to understand them through their thick accents than life in Manila!"

"That is exactly what I am trying to say, Anna. This new environment could come as a complete shock. And Rachel will have to do a lot of adjusting to this new life of hers. She will have very little of the life she has here. She will need to be strong and up for the challenge."

"I know, Mom, and I believe in Rachel. She already knows about the adjustment that she has to do and how she needs to be flexible to survive and succeed. In fact, she told me she has three choices—to be positive, negative, or indifferent. And she also knows which to be so that she can excel especially during this time of extreme change in her life."

"Well, I'm happy for Rachel then and I'm glad she knows that. You should know, too, Anna, that the only opportunity for us to grow comes from change. That's the first rule of flexibility. As it is, change is unavoidable and it is a powerful part of human life. So it's really up to you if you wish to see change as something dark and dreadful or a hopeful answer to a new life. It was William Wadsworth Longfellow who said, 'Lives of great men should remind all of us that we can make our lives sublime and in departing, leave behind us footprints in the sands of time.' "

"Saint Paul also said that whatever we do, we should work at it with all our heart as if we are working for the Lord, and not for men. And unless we do our best, we may never know what we might have accomplished in life," Anna's Mom added.

The two women finally reached Rachel's doorstep. No one seemed to have heard Anna ring the bell so she pushed the door open. She could not see Rachel in the sea of people shouting and singing, "For She's a Jolly Good Fellow." The crowd parted and there was Rachel holding up a big cake in front of her.

Now, Anna completely understood. Change was about to happen. Not just for Rachel, but for her as well. This change, calling itself life direction, has finally arrived.

> Let us, then, be up and doing,
> With a heart for any fate;
> Still achieving, still pursuing,
> Learn to labor and to wait.
>
> —*A Psalm of Life, William Wadsworth Longfellow*

The thunderous applause of the students broke my introspection. I was glad they appreciated my story. I did my best to make sure they could relate to it easily. One student in the back of the room raised a question about cultural acceptance. A valid question, indeed, given that our university is as diverse as it can realistically be here in the Philippines. I cannot speak of any other culture but my own. As it is, I am...

Proud to be Pinoy

It is my hope that even if I speak as a Filipino and share with you my own culture and tradition, my message will touch you whether you are Asian, a Westerner, or of Middle-Eastern descent. After all, we are now citizens of the world.

"When sociologists speak of Filipino cultural values, they identify *asal* as the foundation of *damdamin, dangal*, and *kapwa*. They say, this is what makes a Filipino. *Damdamin* brings about *hiya, amor propio*, and *awa*. *Dangal*, on the other hand, is made up of *pagbabahala, galang*, and *utang na loob*. *Kapwa* brings about *pakikisama, pakikitungo*, and *pakikiramay*."

Time and experience have proven that there is truly a significance and benefit in studying cultural values. Businesses fail to thrive when owners do not succeed in capturing the very essence of what makes both his customers and employees tick. To understand them requires not just management skills, but also a deep-seated knowledge and appreciation of their culture and values.

San Miguel Corporation, for example, understands what Filipino consumers value and what they are willing to spend for. This is apparent in the way they market their food products. And it is this kind of insight that has made

San Miguel Corporation what it is today—a champion in their field.

But it is only when you are in an environment opposed to your own that your value for cultural norms can really be put to test. How far are you willing to stick to your own beliefs and practices in spite of what everybody think? Your answer is as good as a reflection of how you value yourself and your cultural identity. Notice how it is for us, Filipinos, sometimes, especially when it concerns our relationship with Americans. We feel grateful for the West for having paved the way for our liberation and education. And as an appreciative nation that we are, we acknowledge their help in introducing our country to democracy and antislavery. It is through the kindness of the Americans that it is now possible to feel patriotic and nationalistic towards a country we nearly lost to another. Yet paradoxically, we will also willingly give it up anytime especially for the Americans. This, in spite of the fact that Westerners treat Asians and Africans as second-class citizens. We erroneously believe that because we owe them, we owe them our entirety.

In a 1983 study done by a sociologist named Vazquez de Jesus, he found out that Filipinos are basically driven to provide security for their family. We see work as only a means to provide happiness and comfort for the family. Personal ambition and a career are only secondary, if even given any consideration at all. On the other hand, in the West, livelihood is seen as a vehicle for status, recognition, and self-actualization.

And with America's progressive economy, Filipinos can't help but consider the West as a place for employment given our dire need to provide for our family. Imagine then the incongruence this causes in our identity and personal value system. It asks that we accustom ourselves to being driven by career goals first before family and community. That is if we want to make it in the West.

And if we succeed in thinking the way Americans do, we become successful and come home to our family proud of being able to provide for them, a virtue every Filipino hopes for. Thus, we are back to being proud to be *Pinoy* because we can act like Westerners when we are in the West. This seems to be what our cultural identity is.

Fr. Miguel A. Bernard, SJ wrote about inculturation which was published in the *Philippine Star*. According to Fr. Bernard, "The road up and down is one and the same. Inculturation is embedding the Gospel as part of culture and in the same token, adapting the culture to the Gospel." He believes that it is possible to assimilate the best of both religion and culture. In line with this, I'd like to believe that it is the same for two seeming opposing cultures. It is no longer true that the East and West shall never meet. It can certainly be brought together, united in ways and values so that its people can enjoy the best of both worlds.

It is now getting dark. The school custodian has begun making his rounds in the campus. The teacher is ready to go but the students wished for more. Maybe just one more then we should all call it a day.

Beyond the Grade

> Some men see things that are and ask why?
> I see things that never were and ask why not?
>
> —*Northbound Train, Karl Albrecht*

Karl Albrecht defines *Northbound Train* as driving an idea where all resistance crumbles. Filled with metaphor, this term implies two things: purpose and direction.

Vision and mission statements hold no value unless it is motivated by a drive to succeed. Only then will it be read, understood, committed to, and lived by. Albrecht's concept of a moving train conveys momentum and direction, both of which are critical for success. He refers to the Northbound Train as the direction we are headed. One either has to go north or nowhere at all. And Albrecht expects that anyone who decides to join the ride must finish the journey.

That is how it must be for students, the teacher explained. When you aspire for greatness, you need to know how to get *there*. But first, you need to know where *there* is. And in many ways, that is the crisis of today's youth.

In his book *Man's Search for Meaning*, psychologist Victor Frankl expresses his thoughts this way, "As a Jew who survived the Holocaust, I realize that all human beings need a defining purpose to live. There must be something to believe in, something to hope for, and something to strive for.

Those who lost it or never acquire it become dysfunctional at best and criminally maladjusted at worst."

Today, students are called upon not just to deliver good grades but to exemplify strong leadership potentials as well. Education is no longer merely about grades but also one's ability to lead and guide others. Commanding and controlling leadership is out, persuasive leadership is in. As they say after all, you can lead a horse to the water but you can't force it to drink. Leaders these days do not need girth and built, but rather compassion and a compelling ability to be in charge.

And then what, you may ask? Yes, *quo vadis*. Where do we go from here?

> To make a great dream come true,
> you must first have a great dream.
>
> —*Hans Selye*

Dreaming is not as easy as one thinks. Unless, of course, one merely wants to leave it at that and never pursue it. We may have the skills to make it happen. But to make *what* happen is the real challenge. Reconciling what we are today and what we want ourselves to be in the future is the way towards achieving a dream. And no one has ever claimed achieving dreams to be simple.

Recall the story written by Richard Bach entitled *Jonathan Livingston Seagull* where the main character was preoccupied to learning to fly like a falcon when, in fact, he was a seagull.

He tried many times and all those times, he failed. What did he expect? He was dreaming beyond himself. Jonathan felt like a failure. He could not make it as a falcon because he was a seagull. He was lonely and out of place but his heart could not contain itself when one day, he say a falcon fly over him and noticed its wings. The falcon had short wings! That's it! Without a moment to think again, Jonathan positioned himself and clipped his clumsy seagull wings under his chest and fell into a dive. He did it!

The story carries with it several possible interpretations. But I think there will be no argument here when I say that for all its worth, let us recognize Jonathan's strength to break away from what everyone thought he was so he could become what he felt he ought to be. It took courage to push himself to see what he could be made of and he succeeded in doing so. That in itself is honorable.

In Pope John Paul II's book entitled *Prayers and Devotions*, he wrote:

> "In God the Creator and Redeemer's plan, the family not only discovers its identity that which it is, but also discovers its mission, that which it can and ought to do. The task, which the family is called upon by God to accomplish, is derived from its very essence and represents its dynamic and existential development. Every family discovers and finds an irrepressible call in itself. This call defines at once its dignity and its responsibility—for the family to become what it truly was meant to be."

I was shocked by what had just taken place today. I knew I was a storyteller but I didn't think I had it in me to do it in the presence of my own Teacher. I could swear that the Master was speaking through me. And as if reading my thoughts, he said, "David, always remember that, *All wisdom comes from the Lord and with him it remains forever* (Sirach 1:1)."

> *Give me Wisdom, the attendant at your throne,*
> *and reject me not from among your children;*
> *For I am your servant, the son of your handmaid,*
> *a man weak and short-lived*
> *and lacking in comprehension*
> *of judgment and of laws.*
> *Indeed, though one be perfect*
> *among the sons of men,*
> *if Wisdom, who comes from you, be not with him,*
> *he shall be held in no esteem* (Wisdom 9:4-6).

Thank you for making me an instrument of your wisdom.

CHAPTER IV
The Children of Emmaus

Innocent and Confident

They all exude innocence and confidence, in their growing years the adults in their lives will always be there at their side, to love them, to protect them.

The Children of Yesterday

Bible commentators have long agreed that the Good Book has never concerned itself with the joys of childhood. In fact, there are passages in the Bible which seem to imply that children, particularly girls, were considered second-class citizens. It goes as far back as the Old Testament where children of enemies were not even worth running swords on. They were either clubbed to death or thrown from heights.

At worst, as written in Hosea 10:14, a mother was said to have been dashed to pieces upon her children. At best, the children's lives are spared but they're bound to be slaves for life.

True, there were a handful of laws that attempted to protect children but they were not imposed as effectively as one would wish because there were many more that were not beneficial to them. For example, in Deuteronomy 24:16, it was specified that *"Fathers shall not be put to death for their children, nor children for their fathers; only for his own guilt shall a man be put to death."*

Yet again, in the same book (Deuteronomy 23:3), it said, *"No child of an incestuous union may be admitted into the community of the Lord, nor any descendant of his even to the tenth generation."* And if a father is unable to pay his debts, his children could serve as settlement by being enslaved by the creditors. In fact, children were offered as burnt offerings in times of deadly drought, famine, or epidemic. This was so because it was believed that calamities were of God's doing— sent to the world as punishment for some grave sin committed by man.

But all this changed during the time of Jesus.

And now, I am about to hear it straight from him firsthand.

He began:

"It is customary for children of Jews to be presented to a rabbi for blessings. But my disciples' figure for themselves that I had more important things to do than hold wailing children and cradle them in my arms. They were grossly mistaken. I am disappointed because even after spending time with me and listening to my discourses, they still haven't shed their earthly blinders."

"They should have known better. They should have also known that I hear the prayer of mothers about their maternal woes and worries. I know the burden that they carry in their hearts. So I told them, 'Let the children come to me and do not hinder them. It is to them that the kingdom of God belongs. I assure you that whoever does not accept the reign of God like a little child shall not take part in it.' After my disciples shielded the children from me, I just had to embrace each of them, bless them, and place my hands on them."

Such is the love of Jesus for children, a love that came from his Father. Because if you remember the story of the feeding of the multitude, God willed that the food brought by the little boy to the gathering be used by Jesus to be part of his miracle.

The story went as such:

As Jesus delivered his teachings beside the sea, a multitude of people gathered around. They gave him their undivided attention until the sun began to settle down for the day. They have not eaten anything since that morning and Jesus expressed his concern when he asked, "Where shall we buy bread for the people to eat?"

The disciples looked around and saw the impossibility of feeding all who were there. Andrew tried to help and say that there was a little boy who had five barley loaves and a couple of dried fish. But what good is that for so many?

At that point, Jesus could have conjured a sumptuous feast out of nothing. But instead, he chose a little boy for many reasons. One of which is the child's innate selflessness to part with his meager meal and share it with the rest of the crowd. His gesture is a stark reminder that truly, the young provides hope for all of humanity.

But, above all, the miracle of the loaves teaches all of us that all children are God's. They are not properties of their parents or the community but only placed under their responsibility by the Creator… until they become full children of God.

The Children of Today

I, too, have a story that I'd like to share about children. It is about a child that was most loved that died. Her grandfather loved her so much and her parents doted on her endlessly— truly, she was a child of love. And in her passing, she brought so much sadness and among them to a good friend of mine from high school.

Nelson. Nelson. Nelson. My good friend, Nelson. He was so sad that I'm afraid he never recovered from her death. In her death, he now lives a life of sadness.

When my friends from Arellano High School and I finally found each other again through the Internet, there were many happy exchanges and updates about each other's lives. We were drawn to each other like it was yesterday. We laughed and reminisced about life and love until the sad news from Nelson stopped us in our tracks.

To be honest, I don't know Nelson that well. In fact, I hardly spent any time with him in high school. But his letter pierced by heart as it was filled with pain and sadness. Apparently, his granddaughter had died in the US where he is now also based. Nelson may not remember me from high school, but I decided to go ahead and write him a letter, at least from one grandfather to another.

The Teacher was all ears listening to me as I began to recall the letter I wrote:

Dear Nelson,

It's David. We were classmates in high school although I doubt if you still remember me. But just the same, I thought I'd write you a letter to tell you that I read the poems Madeline wrote. In fact, I read it several times and felt the sincerity in her words. How wise she is at such a young age. I know you have other grandchildren, but I have no doubt from your letter that Madeline was your favorite. That little girl sure had a special place in your heart!

I know the pain you spoke of when Madeline passed away. A part of you knows it is for the best, yet at the same time, you hold back full acceptance of God's desire because it is painful and sad. And you are right when you said that death can be a happy occasion. Yet no matter how we rationalize the pain, her absence will still linger for a long time.

A while back, my father also said goodbye. But unlike Madeline, we were not wise. We questioned God's wisdom for taking our father away. He was just 80 and wanted more out of life.

You are hoping that in sharing your sadness with us, it will help you heal. In my case, I needed more than that. To make myself feel better, I wrote a book called A Way of Loving in an attempt to capture the love we had for each other and hoped that because it is now in print, his memory will always be here on earth with me.

Of course, when I started to write it, it was done with reckless abandon. I just needed to pour out my pain and sadness and out came with it anger and blame towards God.

My father's death was very difficult for us. But we eventually came to accept it as the Lord now needs him more than we do. After all, my father was a good electrician and maybe, God needed someone like him to keep the lights in heaven flickering. God cares for every star that falls and Tatay needs to make sure none of them do so from now on.

Madeline is now God's own little star. I am sure she is that one star that's lit every night when you look up in the heavens.

All the best for always,
David

As I ended my story, I looked up to the Master and saw him still waiting in anticipation. Truly, this man knows me so well so I went ahead and said, "Yes, Teacher, I do have another story to tell and this time, it's about the joy of sorrow."

A Rose in the Bush

During the time when I was changing gears in terms of my career, I came upon a Center for the poor. It was an opportunity to do an outreach project for the less fortunate. I wanted to give some relief to a community that was going through difficult times. And as you know, in God's garden where a bush seems to have only thorns, you will be surprised at that one rose that survives in it. And this is one story of such a rose.

From a distance, the houses look like disarrayed stacks of boxes ready for pickup by the garbage truck. These makeshift houses exude a perennial stink that comes from the nearby creek yet the children hardly notice it anymore as they play in the space alongside the bridge. There is smoke coming from the mountain of trash and it hangs like a fog-like mist in their area. It adds loneliness to the already gloomy atmosphere of this place they all call home.

Luzviminda has been waking up to this kind of mornings for years. And as the holidays draw near, there is an added chill in the air. And she relishes it. Above her bed then was a small window that the rays of the sun peeped through. When the sun began to hit her face, it was time to get up and make breakfast. Her father would be waiting for it as he came back home from working since dawn. Her mother would be done with the laundry by this time and would be ironing some clothes. Luzviminda would swing out her legs from her bed and grab for her crutches. This was how it's been.

She then heard her father parking the pushcart. He would at this time be looking forward to his hot coffee and *pandesal*. On a good day in the market, there would be butter in between his bread. On an extraordinary day, there was a can of corned beef or pork and beans. She only found out what kind of day it was when her father stepped in their house.

But regardless of the kind of day it's been, Luzviminda has been blessed with a winsome smile. She has always looked at life as a gift from God. After all, she believes that everything that God gives is good for her. She may be disabled but she sees this as God's way of keeping her close to him. When she fell victim to polio as a child, the doctors said it was too late. But her spirit fought back and willed her to live. That incident would be the hallmark of her entire life.

Luzviminda worked her way through high school doing all kinds of odd jobs. There was Aling Inday who gave her baby dresses to sew once in a while. Or Mang Carding who asked to stack empty bottles in boxes for the junk shop. She even remembers Nanay Ipay who gave her tobacco leaves to roll. She took on those jobs with no second thought. This paved her way to finishing high school. Prayers have always been part of Luzviminda's life. And in her discernment, she gave in to the pleas of a religious house that was looking for a volunteer teacher. They needed someone to manage their nutrition learning program and Luzviminda could not, in her heart, let this calling pass.

The children were an inspiring challenge and they loved her tremendously. There was a little boy who had a deformed foot that had a particular fondness for her. The other children laughed at him but he found strength in Luzviminda seeing that she walked with a crutch but with a smile and her chin held high. The other children stopped their foolishness for fear that they might offend Luzviminda whom they respected dearly.

One day, Fr. Luigi, the head of the learning center, came up to her and asked how she felt about taking up a two-year computer course. Luzviminda was at a loss for words. Tears fell as she gave Fr. Luigi a hug. And like a true gentleman of God, he handed her a tissue and kept his promise.

That was two years ago and now Luzviminda is back in the Center. True to her nature and spirit, she is still a volunteer but now also works as a regular staff member of the congregation.

Fr. Joseph Gabaldon, author of the *Mustard Seed*, wrote about following one's heart. He said that one must build an archway to the heart, with neither lock nor door, and life will pass freely through that archway in harmony with one's senses. He continues, "Love is everywhere. It is in the night sky where stars smile. It is in the field of rice dancing in the wind. It is in the waves sculpturing the rocks. It is in the sound of music, in man's creation of art. It is a seed nourished by two human beings. Love will find you and you will find love— if love becomes your attitude."

Luzviminda followed her heart and because of this, she became a true child of Emmaus.

Caleb and Luke

What is a story about children without talking of my own? I could not wait for the Teacher to hear about some of mine. I began: My son Caleb chose to look for his bright future far away from us. It was a decision that would bring his family some semblance of financial security. And true enough, it did not take long before his business started to flourish. As his venture started growing, he then needed help. And soon, my other son, Luke was on his way to work with his older brother. They were then living the American dream. There was a downside to this dream though. Because of their life choices, I miss their physical presence and the pleasure of spoiling our grandchildren year-round. Because of work schedules, I treasure our rare moments together. And then one day, it just happened. After 20 years, our family was together once again. I kept a written journal so that I can exult in these memories whenever I wished. I'd like to share that with you now.

It happened in America before 9/11. My wife and I were there to visit our sons, Caleb and Luke. Caleb never went back home after graduating in a state university. Luke, on the other hand, gave up his business at home when his *Kuya* needed him to fly back to America to help manage his consulting firm. We were also looking forward to seeing our grandchildren. Caleb's sons were already teenagers and frequently visited Manila but Luke's sons were like strangers to us. They left when they were infants and my wife and I feared that they won't even have any memory of our existence.

When the two young kids met us at the airport, they gave us tight hugs that only innocent children could. But they knew nothing about us but we relished the intimacy just the same. It was a great start. Matt, the younger one, is the talker. Nate is more quiet. So as Matt delighted us with his stories about school and his friends, Nate quietly stared at us. But Luke assured me that it just would take awhile and soon, we would hear from Nate as well.

Golf is what my sons and I have in common. We will all gladly trade it for shopping with our wives, that's for sure.

Besides the competition, the game also has a way of putting us at ease with each other almost immediately. It is like there was no time apart between us. We use the game as a primer to bring out other things to talk about.

Caleb plays the game with an intensity you cannot imagine. He concentrates on his swing as if his life depends on it. And when he makes a perfect shot, he will always want to make sure that I am a witness to it. Of course, he gets a pat on the back from me. The same goes for Luke who will remind him in jest that his good shots are far in between. Caleb plays golf just like the way he works. He is a problem-solver and each swing is a challenge to accomplish. Luke, on the other hand, is a quiet golfer. Like a stream that runs deep, it is hard not to stare, be inspired, and wish it never ends. And like his *Kuya*, he lives his life the way he plays golf. He immerses himself in it completely just like he is towards his wife and children. And his perfect stroke in life is how perfectly well-mannered and polite his children are.

Together with our two lovely daughters living with us in Manila, we are rearing a Christian family and it does not happen by accident. You have to live the virtues that lead to spiritual growth. Fr. Francis Fernandez in his book, *In Conversation with God*, writes:

> "Jesus used different images to teach us the path that leads to Life, to Holiness, in the full development of spiritual life. He speaks of the tiny mustard seed which grows into a great tree; in its branches the birds from the air come to rest. He speaks of the grain of wheat which

reaches maturity and produces rich ears of corn… that growth, not without its difficulties and sometimes seeming so slow, is in fact the increase of virtue."

My wife and I, our entire family actually, try to sanctify each day. We try to live many human and supernatural virtues like faith, hope, and charity. And as we look at our children, we are more than pleased with ourselves as to how they have put their lives to good use for their own families and others.

Let me close with more thoughts from Fr. Fernandez:

"This life of childhood is possible if we have a deep-rooted awareness of being children of God. The mystery of divine filiation, founded on our spiritual life, is one of the consequences of redemption. We are God's children now and it is very important that we become clearly aware of this marvelous reality so that we can approach God with the childlike spirit of a good son."

I praise the Lord for the blessings of my children and their children. And I continue to pray for them as I walk with the man from Emmaus. I walk with him with my children in mind and my grandchildren in my heart.

CHAPTER V
The Women of Emmaus

My Mother, My Sisters, My Friends

The women in the time of the Resurrection can easily be my own mother, my sisters, my friends. They are part of the life that is also the Teacher's life. As you read on, you will find how authentic these women of the past in the many lessons they impart.

*C*leopas excitedly ran towards us as he caught sight of the Teacher and I walking together. He excitedly hugged the Teacher and could not wait to find out how our time together went. The Teacher greeted him and the rest of the disciples. He sounded impressed by what he found out about the children. And how at such a young age, they have already been taught about the man who saved the world from total damnation.

It was then time to talk about the women of their time.

Generally, women then were mere subordinates and shadowy figures of men. It was, no doubt, a man's world. Even Paul, who wrote about the immoralities of Corinth, encouraged the subordination of women. Hebrew women never walked side by side with men. They walked a respectable distance behind them and were carefully covered with a veil from head to foot so as to avoid impropriety. Women's liberation was unheard of during this time. Yet in spite of this practice, there were a number of outstanding women who gained prominence by virtue of character. A few of them were such godly women that they were part of the Master's life during his crucifixion. Of course, the most virtuous of them all is Mary, his own mother.

In the sixth month [of Elizabeth's pregnancy], the angel Gabriel was sent from God to a town of Galilee called Nazareth, to a virgin betrothed to a man named Joseph, of the house of David, and the virgin's name was Mary. And coming to her, he said, "Hail, favored one! The Lord is with you." But she was greatly troubled at what was said and pondered what sort of greeting this might be.

Then the angel said to her, Do not be afraid, Mary, for you have found favor with God. Behold, you will conceive in your womb and bear a son, and you shall name him Jesus. He will be great and will be called Son of the Most High, and the Lord God will give him the throne of David, his father, and he will rule over the house of Jacob forever, and of his kingdom there will be no end (Luke 1:26-33).

Essential to this story is of the equally outstanding decision of the Lord to favor Mary's cousin Elizabeth who was barren in her old age and was married to Zechariah, both devout followers of Jesus. They both lived according to the letter and the spirit of the law. One day, the angel Gabriel appeared to Zechariah and announced that God had heard their prayers. After years of prayers and pleadings, they have finally been given an offspring. Elizabeth and Zechariah realized that God meant for them to have a special son, one who will test their patience and faith. And they also realized that with God, certainly nothing was impossible!

And then the Teacher continued:

"But Mary said to the angel, 'How can this be, since I have no relations with a man?' And the angel said to her in reply, 'The holy Spirit will come upon you, and the power of the Most High will overshadow you. Therefore, the child to be born will be called holy, the Son of God. And behold, Elizabeth, your relative, has also conceived a son in her old age, and this is the sixth month for her who was called barren; for nothing will be impossible for God.' Mary said, 'Behold, I am the handmaid of the Lord. May it be done to me according to your word.' Then the angel departed from her" (Luke 1:34-38).

God even gave Elizabeth's son his name—John!

The man called Jesus, the son of Mary, had many friends. Among them was Martha, the sister of Lazarus who was raised from the dead. Many times, she was a gracious hostess to Jesus and his disciples when they visited Bethany. On one particular evening though, they came rather unexpectedly and Martha was visibly irritated and peeved. While she was busy darting in and out of their kitchen preparing food for the guests, her sister Mary was unmindful of the pending tasks. Instead, she was mesmerized by the Master to even offer to help. Bursting in full smoldering anger, Martha blurted out, *"Lord, do you not care that my sister has left me by myself to do the serving? Tell her to help me"* (Luke 10:40).

This was not the first time that Martha could accuse Jesus. The second time was when Lazarus had just been buried for four days. While the household was full of comforting friends,

Martha came up to Jesus immediately when he arrived and chided, *"Lord if you had been here, my brother would not have died"* (John 11:21).

But quickly realizing her arrogance, she expressed her wholehearted confession of faith. *"[But] even now I know that whatever you ask of God, God will give you"* (John 11:22).

Martha's final retort was an unmistakable and most profound confession of faith, *"Yes, Lord. I have come to believe that you are the Messiah, the Son of God, the one who is coming into the world"* (John 11:27).

There is a female equivalent of Lazarus, who was a special friend of Jesus. Her name was Dorcas, Greek for Tabitha. She was way ahead of any woman in the Bible which accounts for the seven people who were raised from the dead. Dorcas was the only female among them. She was also the only female called a disciple.

Dorcas has been a follower of Jesus for some time. She received him as her redeemer and her faith has been more than just fellowship with God. She used this as a tool for serving others. Dorcas was an excellent seamstress—a God-given talent that she put to good use in his name. She made clothes for free and gave it to the widows and orphans of Joppa (now known as Jaffa), a place along the Mediterranean where the main source of livelihood was fishing. During extreme weather, many fishermen were shipwrecked and lost their lives.

As a disciple of Jesus, Dorcas heeded his admonition to take care of the widows and orphans. Because of her, many of them were shielded from the heat of the sun and from the biting winter cold. Dorcas understood their loneliness and sadness and was able to console them of their grief. Because of this, she became a prominent personality in the Church. Practically the whole of Joppa was saddened and felt desolate with Dorcas' untimely death.

The apostle, Peter, was in nearby Lydda from where he was fetched by two men from Joppa. The town has heard about Peter's miraculous deeds and wished that he could perform one for their beloved Dorcas. When Peter arrived in the room where Dorcas' body lay, he asked the people that gathered around to leave him alone with her. Peter then kneeled down and prayed aloud, *"Tabitha [Dorcas], rise up"* (Acts 9:40).

She opened her eyes and when she saw Peter, Dorcas sat up. Then Peter called the crowd in, including the widows and presented her to them. This time she was alive. The life, death, and resuscitation of Dorcas helped the rapid spread of the Gospel immensely. She, too, can be aligned with the other great evangelists.

David looked upon the Teacher and noticed that he looked tired. As the Teacher took a short nap, David appreciated the sights. He found a comfortable spot under the shade and looked at the pleasant greenery until the Teacher called him again to continue his narration.

There was a woman, not named in the Bible, but was only known as the one by Jacob's well. She chose to draw water from the well at noontime. She endured the heat of the sun and refused to do it any other time when it was cooler. It was because she was a woman of seeming bad reputation. She drew water at the worst time of the day so that no one else will be there as she was a rich fodder for gossip.

One day, she saw a man sitting by the well. Immediately, she recognized him as a Jew. He looked tired and her natural impulse was to turn away and leave. She especially knew that Jews like him shunned Samaritans like her.

"Give me a drink" (John 4:7), the man said. It sounded like a plea of help, a favor. The woman was completely taken aback. Wasn't it forbidden for Jewish men to talk to women on the street, especially nicely and politely? And after all, Jews and Samaritans do not share the same cups and bowls!

The woman, with much hesitation, replied, *"How can you, a Jew, ask me, a Samaritan woman, for a drink?"* (John 4:9).

As if not hearing her, the man replied, *"Everyone who drinks this water will be thirsty again; but whoever drinks the water I shall give will never thirst; the water that I shall give will become in him a spring of water welling up to eternal life"* (John 4:13-14).

The woman's heart raced. This is the kind of water she has been looking for! If she can have it, she will never have to draw water from the well again. She will never have to endure the scorching afternoon sun to quickly lug her heavy jug of water back home while dreading the jeers of the gossipers. Unfortunately, the woman had not caught on the real, deeper message of the man, the Jew named Jesus. Upon realizing this, all the waters on earth could not have quenched the dryness in her throat. What she needed was her parched soul to be doused with Jesus' *living water*. Her heart and soul needed cleansing. After all, she was a woman of ill-repute. Known to have shared her bed with at least five different men, she remained unmarried. And upon her honesty about who she really was, she realized that the man already knew about her. And yet, he remained and spoke to her, not at all shunning her. This man is indeed a prophet, she concluded. He saw beyond her form and appreciated her religious beliefs and practices. *"I know that the Messiah is coming, the one called the Anointed; when he comes, he will tell us everything"* (John 4:25), the woman said to herself. And at this moment, Jesus knew that his purpose for meeting this woman has been achieved. He then declared, *"I am he [the Messiah], the one who is speaking with you"* (John 4:26).

Wait a minute, David said to himself. I read the Bible daily and know it better than most. I don't remember that line being contained in the Bible. But I'm quite sure during this time; the woman was embraced with both awe and humility. The Messiah has come a long way to manifest himself to this sinful woman who thought that life was hopeless and empty. He has come to show his love and understanding and now, all her sins have been forgiven.

I now recall that it is this same woman, who because of her experience, ran to the nearest town to invite the others to come and meet the Prophet. Her sins have been absolved and she has been granted a new life. And because of this, she no longer carried shame towards anyone. When the other Samaritans came upon her invitation, they met Jesus and begged him to stay. It is this Samaritan woman's selfless gesture of sharing her encounter with the Messiah that began the evangelistic movement in Samaria.

I wondered though about the women who were truly the outcasts of society. Those mentioned so far are blessed—gifted with the ability to relate to the Master's teachings. But what about those who seem to have been forgotten by the Lord? Does he favor one from the other? Is he selective in his love for his people?

As if reading my mind, the Master said, "That needs more understanding of the nature of the Lord, David. But let me attempt to explain it to you."

Jerusalem has always been the center of frantic activities when Passover draws near. A devout Jew will not miss this important celebration in the Holy City. In a Jewish home, for example, most women are busy preparing the Passover meal. This is for families who are fortunate enough to be able to purchase all the allowable meat and fowl as well as condiments and spices, of course. Those who do not have much pass up this celebration because they have to prioritize the regular sustenance of their families. Except for this one particular widow.

St. Mark and St. Luke in their respective Gospel narratives singularly honored her with a stirring account of how she was unable to prepare a feast for the Passover celebration yet she did the best thing she could in her situation. She went straight to the Temple and approached the offering box. And as inconspicuously as possible, she dropped her last two copper coins, still moist from the sweat of her tightly closed fist. She tried to hide her miniscule contribution from the rest. Truly a sacrificial gift from a faithful follower who was not even certain when her next meal would be.

As quietly as she came in was how quietly she planned to leave. Or so she thought.

But Jesus was at the temple; he saw her and what she did. He called the attention of his disciples to this sincere act of love for her God. He said, *"Amen, I say to you, this poor widow put in more than all the other contributors to the treasury. For they have all contributed from their surplus wealth, but she, from her poverty, has contributed all she had, her whole livelihood"* (Mark 12:43-44). (See also Luke 21:1-4).

Clearly, Jesus saw beyond the monetary value of the two small coins. What was more valuable was how much the widow was left with after her contribution—nothing! As a Jew, she was bound by the Old Testament decree for tithing—10% of all income for the temple. But she was not happy with just 10%, instead she gave 100%, fully trusting that God would take care of her. She knew in her heart that she won't be disappointed.

And then there was this woman who had been suffering from hemorrhage for a long, difficult twelve years. She had spent almost all that she had in consultation with all sorts of doctors. But one was able to make her well. Even Saint Mark bluntly took to task some of the physicians who took advantage of her and made her feel worse about herself. When she heard that Jesus was coming to visit Galilee, she hoped to be able to meet him. Communities far and wide have already heard of the miracle cures of Jesus, she hoped to be touched by him. When Jesus arrived in Galilee, an official of the local synagogue named Jarius begged him to come to his house. His only daughter was dying. On his way there, a great mass of people were following him and it was getting harder and harder to move and walk forward. Among the throngs of people was the diseased woman. But she was too weak to move closer to him. It was the push and shoves of the crowd that helped move her and fortunately, it was towards him. She was too weak to even stand on her own.

After a while, she found herself so near him yet still unable to reach out. She did not think she can make it any closer; all she hoped was that she would be able to touch even his garment. And with all the faith and hope that she could muster, she stretched herself for what may be the last time she could. She was able to slightly touch the end of his cloak!

But she wasn't the only one. There were hundreds, if not thousands, of people doing the same. Some of them grabbed on his sleeve, some from behind him. But this woman's touch was different. It had the intensity of pure faith and devotion that her bleeding stopped upon contact.

Jesus then spun around and asked his disciples, *"Who touched me?"* None of them did. Until Peter said, *"Master, the crowds are pushing and pressing in upon you."* Jesus replied, *"Someone has touched me; for I know that power has gone out from me"* (see Luke 8:43-46).

When the woman heard that she has been found out, she came forward, trembling in fear. She feared that Jesus might drive her away just like what he did to the vendors of the temple grounds. She threw herself on the ground and on his feet. Still trembling and in between sobs, she explained why she had to touch him. And that upon their contact, how she believed she has been healed. The woman, with her head still down, felt hands touching her ever so gently. She slowly looked up and saw Jesus helped her get up on her feet. The crowd watched in awe. Silence befell everyone. *"Daughter, your faith has saved you; go in peace"* (Luke 8:48). These were the last words Jesus spoke to her before she walked away.

Interestingly, these people with amazing stories are not named in the Bible. Their stories are told but their identities are not revealed. It is God's way of telling us that these stories are not just theirs, but may be ours as well.

Cleopas turned to me and waited in anticipation. It took awhile for me to realize that they were waiting for my share of stories about women of the 21st century.

How do I begin to explain to them that being a woman nowadays is so different from what they know? Most women are now on equal terms with men, if not even higher. In fact, some countries honor women more than men.

Cleopas looked at me. It was too difficult for them to fathom how women's lives have changed over time. The only way I could make them understand is to explain it the way the Master did—through real life experiences and stories.

But I had to assure Cleopas that the women of today are just as simple, just as sweet, and even just as self-sacrificing as the women of their time. The only way for them to believe is by letting them meet the women closest to my heart.

CHAPTER VI
The Emmaus Women of Today

Women of Today

Sharing with you the story of the women of today is a most pleasant task for me. I had the chance to put in print this burning love they have gifted me with so much, and even as I have their love, you will want to keep the lesson they so willingly give.

$\mathcal{I}$t's been a long day, but not nearly enough. The mid-afternoon sun burned our backs and we were nearing a fork on the road. The way to Emmaus was on the right but it was time to take a break. We were all exhausted and thirsty. The Teacher saw a group of women coming down the hill. "Maybe the woman coming upon us can share water to drink," he said. Our water has been long gone and we needed something to cool ourselves.

One of the disciples who has been silent all throughout our journey offered some leftover wine. But the Teacher replied, "No, thank you. The sun must have warmed the alcohol in the wine. That will make all of us drowsy. Let's wait, surely the women will have water to spare. My own mother never leaves home without a reserve of water."

So we all waited. Quietly. Patiently. Hopeful. As the women came nearer, Cleopas greeted them loudly, "Good morning, ladies. May the presence of the Lord be upon you."

The older woman replied, "Hail and good tidings be with you, too," as she bowed a little as a sign of respect. Her other companions looked at us and smiled. I could not help myself any longer so I said, "Excuse me, mother, I hope you don't mind me calling you that. We have been walking since the break of dawn and have not had any drink. Would you be so kind as to share some water? Our Teacher in particular needs some."

The young lady came up and said, "We have enough water. May I bring out the cups?" she asked looking at her mother for permission.

"Go ahead, child," the older lady said.

Cleopas asked them if they were on their way to Jerusalem. Apparently, yes.

They identified themselves as the followers of the Man the Romans crucified three days ago. They were going to visit the tomb of the Master, clean it up, and plant some flowers. One of the other disciples excitedly chimed in, "Can you believe it? That is exactly what we have been talking about all morning! Some of the women in our group reported that the tomb is empty. We don't believe it yet until we see it for ourselves. Besides, if our Master was taken away, surely, the men who have been with the Master all this time would be the first to know with all due respect to you, Mother."

I wasn't quite sure where this was going. "Mother, I am from another time and have read that the Master was taken by the guards. None of his apostles can be seen. Could it be that the Master is honoring the women of Emmaus by allowing them to see him first on the very day that he resurrected? We know that in the hour when he needed them most, it was the women of Emmaus that lent their presence, fear not in their hearts but love for the suffering Messiah."

The Teacher interrupted and said, "You may be right, David, but the Master is a righteous person. He will never have any recriminations toward his apostles. He knows all the things that happened to him is preordained by the Father, even this incident of his resurrection where the woman saw him first."

"What does preordained by the Father mean?" I asked.

"God made a covenant with his people. Somewhere along the way, this covenant was broken. The people loved God so much yet they sinned against the Father's commandments. He promised he will never destroy the world again as much as he did during the time of Noah. And so he sent his only Son, this man you call the Master, to save you all."

Cleopas volunteered his concern, "That is what we worry about, would the Father still want to bring us back to his fold, after the way we treated his messenger?"

Therefore, let us be on our guard while the promise of entering into his rest remains, that none of you seem to have failed (Hebrews 4:1). All he asks is that they (Israelites), too, should arise and tell their sons that they should set their hope in God and never forget his deeds. And to keep all of his commands.

"Every day of our lives, we pray for God's deliverance, the Master has shown us the way. It's just too bad that the

Pharisees and the scribes hated him so much and made the Romans the instruments to the Messenger's death," the older woman said in between sobs.

The Teacher assured her and the rest of the group, "I know God has many more good days for us."

"David," the Teacher, changing the subject, asked, "as we are already in the company of women, why don't you tell us about the women of your time?"

I did not know where to begin. But I just knew for sure that women have gone a long way. I myself have traveled through joy and pain in my search for life's meaning and through it all, my wife and my daughter were with me. Together, we have walked through life's roads and have met a few people along the way. And it is these poignant experiences that have helped me capture what the essence of a woman is and why they have become my women of Emmaus today.

I took this opportunity to read to them a letter my daughter once wrote. I have carried it with me wherever I go.

A Letter from Lara

Dear friends,

My father is a weaver of time. He brings people back and forth into his dreams. And in those journeys, I personally saw how his dreams never broke. They simply transform into something that *was meant to be. And if we are fortunate enough to be like him, it might happen to us, too. You have all made it possible for him to be that way.*

His books and articles are your gifts to him. In sharing his stories and life journeys with you, you have all given him so much more than what you are taking away. My father had many great teachers in his life. But I have been privileged to only have one. He has taught me about love and pain, laughter and sadness, and death. He taught me to learn what family means, why sincere friendship is beyond value, why a smile is important to just about anyone, and, above all, what it means to honor your own country. His dreams have become mine and now they are yours as well. And it is in tribute to my father that I celebrate my life today.

One of the happiest moments of my Tatay was the day he and my Nanay walked the aisle once again to celebrate their 40th wedding anniversary. That celebration and the memories of their love flood my mind until today. As they stood before the altar renewing their vows, my Tatay's raspy voice came clearly throughout the Church. He did not say, "I do." Instead, he happily recited the poem, "Roses Speak to me of Love," a love poem he especially composed for my Mom. Everyone responded with applause. We all clapped and cheered. We all got carried away with the moment.

And now, we are the beautiful ideal of that love.

Lara

I never had to worry about Lara. Never mind that she is a girl faced with biases and discrimination because of her gender. My Lara is made of different stuff. In fact, she has always been as aggressive as her two brothers. And if I had something to worry about her, it would probably be her reckless abandon. Lara can get into anything she puts her mind into. She will do well with flying colors. But sometimes, she will also crash to the ground. As a young child during the day, she biked, swam, and ran side by side with her brothers. At night, she sleeps with her doll collection. And oh... how she could read through me. She knew just how to get me to say yes to all that she wished for.

I remember once when she was in high school and she had gone on their annual spiritual retreat. The activity was to conclude by way of a love letter for them from their fathers. She wrote me a touching letter that I was barely halfway reading when I found myself teary-eyed. My little girl was begging me for more time with her. And she wanted me to know why I don't hug her anymore. She also missed the little things we used to do together.

Oh, my Lara. My sweet Lara. In her adolescent years, she still wanted me to tuck her in bed at night and read her a story before she falls asleep. I was also the one she'd call for in the middle of the night during a bad dream. She and I were so much alike especially when it came to our feelings.

Lara had her share of naughtiness and mischief, too. I remember the countless times she would ask me to get her a glass of water in the middle of the night when she's running a fever. Although I knew it was good for her fever, I couldn't help but steal a glance at her playful smile when I had to get up again for that unending "last" glass of water in the wee hours of the morning.

I will never forget that letter she wrote. Since then, I made sure to give her all the hugs I could muster, whether she asks for it or not. Her hugs have become the keys to my heart as well. I don't think I've never said no to her for anything ever since that time! And I dreaded the day that she will grow up and live her own ways. I knew my Lara was mine alone, but I also knew it won't be for long.

Lara is a woman with a gift of a prophet. She can read you like she owns your mind. She is as clever, as loving, and as strong-willed as her mother. She often told people, "I may have gotten my strength from Mom, but mine is different." That's because Lara's resilience also has the gentlest counterpart—a virtue my wife, Sophia, is now beginning to borrow from our daughter.

There are many beautiful stories that flow between my wife and my daughter. I particularly remember the time when they won the most coveted Halloween trophy in our village. You may not believe it, but my wife and daughter take Halloween and the village celebration with all seriousness. Our house is prepped for that one day where residents in our village gawk at the spooky houses while we threw candies and treats their way.

On that particular Halloween day, I found myself scared of my own house. They had placed a coffin in the garage with candles in every corner. I can still hear the haunting melody of Gounod's *Ave Maria* that they played in the background.

There were images of ghosts hanging in our trees that I could barely recognize our own lawn. To add to the morbid scene, Lara had asked her husband Patrick to dress like a London guard and stand by our gate. One of our adopted children from Batangas dressed up like a priest while Sophia was in a witch's costume. Lara wore her dazzling Snow White dress. Cars stopped outside our house to look while people took pictures endlessly. Neighbors also threw in their good wishes that we get the trophy that year. And we did. Actually, Lara did. She was the one that made it all happen. These are the things that are sacred to her, traditions that celebrate her relationship with her mother.

And it's just like Lara to always remind me how proud she is of my love affair with her Mom. In fact, she knew her mother well enough that Sophia wanted something special for our 40th anniversary. After all, forty years of married life is a rarity nowadays. A renewal of vows was what she wished for. And as usual, Lara can make it happen for us.

Not that easy as she thought though. Because apparently, I was too oblivious and insensitive during that time to realize that they were serious about the renewal of vows. In fact, I never took it seriously and even made a joke out of it when they brought it up. I had cracked a joke about marrying her again as long as it wasn't in the Catholic Church. Evidently, I was the only one who thought that was funny. Lara was exasperated and so was my wife. I, on the other hand, was being a moron and didn't even realize it. Lara then feared the emotional fallout that appeared to be taking place between my wife and I as our anniversary plans begin to falter. This time Lara was more determined than ever to have a renewal of vows ceremony and a concrete reminder of our commitment to unconditional love. You know what I mean, that kind of love that gives nothing but itself and takes nothing from itself. And so Lara worked on it and again, she made it happen.

Forty years in one night. Every minute measured. No second missed. Every wink of an eye was like a wisp of the wind. A lifetime of love.

The Holy Family Chapel is a quaint little church near our village. Sophia and I pass by it every day after breakfast in McDonald's but never really noticed it. Not until it became a part of our story and now, that quaint little church occupies a big part of our married life.

It happened on a cool day in December. The green leaves sparkled like lights and the yellow ones that hesitated to fall from the tree and begged for one more day stood watching our love affair unfold in front of family and friends in this quaint little church. Sophia was walking in her magnificence beside Caleb who walked like a handsome prince beside his mother. That day, Sophia was a picture of the same beauty that I took to the altar forty years ago. She had the same smile, the same twinkle in her eyes, and the same casual nods to her friends in the pews as she gazed ahead searching for me. Splendid in her gown, a veil covering her face, it was like she floated to me once again just like it was forty years ago. And that day, I felt like the young man in Paco Church once again, giddy about the life ahead.

To be honest, I hesitated this renewal of marriage vows thing that my daughter and wife wanted. Don't get me wrong.

Ours is a marriage made in heaven. It's been all about love in our love affair. A love that has endured time and everything else in between. And to have to renew it made me think— Did I miss something that had to be reminded to me again? And in front of God? What went wrong? Didn't I do right by my wife? For some reason, I had this notion that a renewal of marriage vows was for relationships that were weak and needed a recharge, that's why. It was Lara who helped me realize that renewing our vows was actually a celebration of our marriage and a way of thanking the Lord for being there and keeping us together.

The other night, while Sophia and I watched TV, I whispered to her playfully, "Do you want to do something exciting tonight?" She was thrilled. This was an unusual moment of vigor especially this late in the night. She said yes and looked at me expectantly. I said, "*Palit tayo ng lugar.* Let's change sides in the bed tonight." Sophia had tears in her eyes from laughing.

These are the little things that Lara wanted us to always remember and preserve. We needed to keep getting married until we perfected the ceremony. Let the celebration of marriage always be second nature to our relationship. Putting the ring on each other's fingers over and over and repeating our marriage vows will keep sealing our love for each other, now and forever.

As I once again stood with Sophia before the Monsignor who was witnessing our marriage, I sealed my vow with a love offering:

Roses Speak to Me of Love

The red roses ooze with youngish freshness /
Mimicking the softness of teenage lips, /
Wet, scented, retreating in the cool touch
of raindrops drip,
dripping from a grayish sky. /
Still, I feel a haunting sigh of petals
gently flowing like freckles loosened
from memories gone by. /
The roses came in three's
softly singing, whispering, murmuring,
my tongue-tied mouth
dreams only of saying,
to a beauty my love immortalized.

Our family album is filled with pages and pages of significant memories that forget nothing and forgive everything. It is the life we have built together and I can only wish the same for all of you. And as a final thought, let me share with you another letter from Lara:

Dear Dad,

You have inspired me to greatness. And now you have done the same to your readers.

Through your soulful words and thoughts, you have made my life sweeter. And because of that, I will always be grateful. My children and my children's children will read your work and

continue your commitment to life and love. And
for that, I love you.

Always,
Lara

Lara was born to please, to make one appreciate the beauty of life and have a heart that cares. I smile because I see Lara in me. Even as time slips away.

And then there was silence. I saw the old woman with misty eyes.

"I would love to have a daughter like Lara, too. This love that you speak of is not easy to find, how lucky you are," said the old woman.

Cleopas added, "I am impressed with Lara. I never had a daughter but should I have one, I hope she would be as loving as your Lara. I am sure your wife is even more, David."

Of course, Cleopas is right. Lara's loving heart takes after her own mother, Sophia.

Bahay Maria

Sophia has been my source of strength. She is the one that helps me survive the challenges that come my way. I learned to live only because of her love. In closeness, we move as one. And I will be lost without her.

When she agreed to marry me, she risked everything she held dear to her—her families, her friends, her security, even her respectability. She said yes to me, not fully knowing where our life together will bring her. But God blessed us. Together, we grew in our love for each other and learned to work things out, mostly on our own. Through the years, Sophia transformed into a creative artist and it all happened in our farm... I was shocked. I didn't expect the chapel to be grand and monumental. But there it stood in the middle of our farm, majestic and special in the middle of simplicity. But then again, I suppose I shouldn't be extremely surprised since Sophia never got into a project that didn't turn out well. But truth be told, it's been awhile since she planned to have catechism classes in the farm. I thought she had forgotten about it or let go of her plans because of her busy schedule. She had been missing her regular prayer lessons with the children from the farm because of numerous errands, adding to that her recent involvement in the projects of the sisters of the Holy Family of Nazareth.

Before she started her prayer sessions with the children, she debated whether to hold it in the Barangay chapel or just in our farm. She eventually preferred the chapel because it helped the children focus on their spirituality. She wanted to renovate the chapel but feared that the *manangs* might misunderstand her intentions. I remember casually consoling her by saying she should consider building her own. I didn't think of it after that. But I guess she did. Because now standing before me in my own farm is a chapel built by Sophia.

She had no professional help. She worked only with her dream, her heart, and those she trusted in our farm.

She took the time to review several pictures of churches all over the world and created her own from them. Armed with determination, she sketched the chapel she envisioned even before the sun rose in the morning. Her adrenalin flowed like never before. I couldn't believe it was the Sophia that I knew.

And then the roof posed a problem. It would cost half of her budget. I suggested a flat roof with tiles. It was going to be economical yet still blend with the baroque facade that she has been aiming for. But it wouldn't work out. We feared losing the sanctity of the chapel. As we continued to brainstorm, one of our trusted help suggested that we use antique-looking bricks, they were cheap and available. And he was right. Now this chapel before me looks like one from Emmaus, if I may say so myself.

From a distance, it looks like a regular church. Its adobe stone finish gives a massive appearance yet picturesque in its real nature. The facade is faithful to the Paoay Church in Ilocos whose history goes back to the Spanish times. Yet when you go inside, it feels like the different missions in California. Bahay Maria is what we named our chapel. She named it that while I thought of it, too. That's how it is with us; we think and say the same things most of the time. The chapel's interior is simplicity defined. There are no walls on the sides, to welcome the gentle winds of our farm. The window panes are colorful and playful, inviting anyone who wishes to while their time away inside. A dated Holy Family carving hangs on one side across the image of Our Lady of Guadalupe. A Santo Niño image stands beside her with a rough wooden crucifix. The natural light gives enough radiance and brilliance that when you are inside, you truly feel the presence of the Lord.

While the chapel was being built, the garden around was also reborn. Many of our plants and decor from our house in the city were brought here to add to the landscape that was forming before our very eyes. The Grotto of Our Lady of Fatima now dominates the scenery.

What drove Sophia to build this chapel? She simply wanted more people in our farm to connect with Jesus through the Holy Family. For Sophia, the Holy Family is built and founded on true love. Remember, Mary says yes to God in obedience and love. Joseph stands by Mary out of love and obedience to God's will. Jesus is obedient to Joseph and Mary out of love for them and for his Father in heaven. Mary is patient and conscientious in raising Jesus whom she loves with all her heart. In Calvary, Mary suffers terribly upon seeing her son on the cross but remains obedient to God's plan… all for love (*365 Days with the Lord*).

Saint Jose Maria Escriva, in his book *Furrow* says, "Some people know nothing about God because no one has talked about him in terms they can understand."

Sophia's touch is for people to know God better. Sounds like the touch of Jesus in Emmaus, doesn't it?

Cleopas, in his usual joyful mood, spoke before I could finish. "I am amazed at how Sophia has created an atmosphere of love in this place you call *Bahay Maria*. God has looked with favor on her lowliness and the Holy Spirit has guided her every action. You and Sophia are truly blessed by the Lord."

The Teacher added, "You are lucky to be living in a time that God has reserved for people of faith, where man has accepted the equality of woman, and women with all humility placed them in the table of love where both man and woman exist. In this time, religion has separated man from God; man is pitted against man, woman against man. Some teachings even emphasize that man is above woman, even as we listen in synagogues that God is above man. Thus the greatest travesty upon woman is perpetuated."

We really are fortunate. The history of humankind has reached us and we recognize the climax of a new beginning with the understanding that the apex of man's existence is with the birth of a child in Bethlehem because *when the fullness of time had come, God sent his Son, born of a woman, born under the law* (Gal 4:4).

I continued on with another story of a woman I felt could be one from Emmaus. I've known her since high school but lost touch along the way. In fact, when she called me a few years back asking about our homecoming, I could barely remember who she was. It took awhile before I recalled Anita.

Aah, Anita. I barely knew her even in high school. We moved in different crowds although I'm quite sure our paths have crossed in school. We rekindled our friendship only when we were planning our high school reunion. It was Anita that got all of us back together again through the internet. She was persistent in coordinating everyone to make sure they were at the homecoming when it happens. And it was because of these friendships that she rebuilt that we are now planning our golden reunion happening in a few years. It was also through Anita's website that my second book, *Bayanihan: The Many Great Lessons of United Laboratories, Inc.* received good publicity and orders were shipped for distribution among our classmates in the U.S.

No one would have expected what her life used to be if you meet her just now. Today, she is a woman of the world. Enjoying all the comforts of life through travels, the theater, and even occasionally, the casino! You'd be surprised how far along she's come because her entire school life was a struggle. She did not even hope for college. There just wasn't enough money for that. Her father was the neighborhood's tailor who could barely make ends meet. Anita had to help complete his orders so a social life in high school was non-existent. Her meager income helping her father was reserved for school expenses. She worked every waking hour when she wasn't in school. Exam week was the worst. Not because she wasn't ready to take them, but mostly because there was the test permit she had to acquire. And that meant working doubly hard to make sure she wasn't behind school payments. On occasion, her friends pitched in to cover the balance of her tuition. Anita kept a record of every centavo a friend gave and made sure each one got back what they gave. She never lived on handouts. That's the kind of person she was. She had unbelievable perseverance.

Knowing how well she focused on her priorities, I was quite surprised to learn that at an early age, Anita was involved in a failed marriage. And then it would appear that her luck had finally changed when she was offered a job at a U.S. military base. An American seaman fell in love with her and she once again hoped for a fairy tale story. Fortunately, the second time around, she got her happy ending.

Ed was a loving husband and spoiled Anita tremendously. He treated Anita's children from her early marriage much like his own. "I love those you love," he would always tell Anita. And for the first time, she knew how it is to be truly loved. And her high school friends, me included, saw this in her e-mails as well. Love poured out of her and it spilled on all of us. We were all happy for Anita. She finally got the life she deserved. It was like she built a neighborhood *sari-sari* store in cyberspace. People hung around her for stories and updates and we all wanted a bit of her time when it came to e-mails. Because of her, more and more people even outside our class were getting together on the internet. Everything she touched grew beautifully. She created closeness in our long distances and has erased time between all of us. Class '55 is back like it was just yesterday that we were together in Math class.

I find my personal friendship with Anita enjoyable. Much like connecting with someone in the village of Emmaus. It is a gracious and joyful meeting, much blessed by the Lord.

The Teacher said, "If only we all see wisdom and clarity of the truth you speak of, then the world would be a better place. May we all learn that what you do for others are the things you want others to do to you. And what others fail to do must be returned with greater affection. If only. If only."

Yes, Lord. If only.

It was time to go. I thanked the older woman for her kind words and bid her daughter goodbye.

CHAPTER VII
Old Friends, Old Wines of Emmaus

Old Friends, Old Wines

They say friendship is like old wine, they taste better with age!

$\mathcal{A}$s we continued our trek to Emmaus, I noticed some vines that were laden with abundant fruits. Cleopas must have seen me looking because he said, "Did you know that there is a story behind why we carry our wine in new wineskins? It is in the book you call the Bible but let me go ahead and tell it to you."

> Then the disciples of John approached him and said, "Why do we and the Pharisees fast [much], but your disciples do not fast?" Jesus answered them, "Can the wedding guests mourn as long as the bridegroom is with them? The days will come when the bridegroom is taken away from them, and then they will fast. No one patches an old cloak with a piece of unshrunken cloth, for its fullness pulls away from the cloak and the tear gets worse. People do not put new wine into old wineskins. Otherwise the skins burst, the wine spills out, and the skins are ruined. Rather, they pour new wine into fresh wineskins, and both are preserved" (Matthew 9:14-17).

David chimed in, "The story of friendship you describe in analogy to the filling of wine in fresh skin or patching an old clothes with new might as well be the friendship between the roots of the vine to the soil of the earth. Without the earth nursing the root, wine will not be produced. In life, some friendships are like this, just like my friendship with Simon. I am sure you will like him, but before I tell you more about Simon, let me share with you some of my thoughts about wine. Because it is in old wine that I came to appreciate my old friend, Simon."

There are many interesting stories that I have learned about raising grapes. Most will tell you that it is much like raising babies. Even if good water is available, you have to control the drip to the wine's roots so that the tree does not go into shock. The roots must be disciplined enough to provide only water to its trunk and branches. No more, no less. This is how to manage good quality grapes.

This art of perfecting wine has been around since the early 6,000 BC. Eastern Europe and the Middle East were the pioneers in drinking wine. If you will remember in the Bible, it was Noah who saved the world during the great deluge. While he stayed close to the Lord's teaching, his contemporaries were eating, drinking, and being merry. And guess what they were drinking? Wine, of course.

Wine and religion have always been tightly intertwined. In the Christian religion, it is seen regularly in the Mass during the liturgy of the Eucharist. Likewise, it is in the Kiddush of the Jewish ceremony. The role of the "blood of the grapes" (also called fermented juice) is seen in many ritual or ceremonies in the Bible. For example, it can be said that the first great biblical figure who was intoxicated from wine excesses was Noah (Genesis 9:20-21). Again in Genesis 19:31-36, an excessive portion of the wine served as the tool for Lot's daughters to successfully carry on the scheme with their own father as the unwitting accomplice. In a more sublime event, Jesus reluctantly performed his miracle at the irresistible behest of his Mother. During a wedding in Cana, when the supply of wine ran out, Jesus turned ordinary water into good wine. The greatest of all wine events was during the Passover. At the Last Supper, *[Jesus] took a cup, gave thanks, and gave it to them, saying, "Drink from it, all of you, for this is my blood of the covenant, which will be shed on behalf of many for the forgiveness of sin. I tell you, from now on I shall not drink this fruit of the vine until the day when I drink it with you new in the kingdom of my Father"* (Matthew 26:27-29). This marked the practice of Communion in the celebration of the Eucharist in Christian Churches.

There are so many interesting facts about wine in our time. Did you know that finding good wine is a lifetime's work for the *aficionados*?

Cleopas interrupted, "David, you know so many things about wine, but I bet you didn't know that in Northern Israel, on the other side of the junction from the old church, on Ramalah Road, is a vineyard?"

I wasn't all that surprised because I knew that Emmaus was known for its wine. But since we're on the subject, I'd like to speak not of the wine per se but the concept of wine as a symbolism of life. Like wine, our life struggle can be sweet, sour, bitter, or maybe dry just like a bottle of wine. But the point is to endure and persevere. Life, like wine, has many cycles. We all have our ups and downs yet no matter what life brings you, you just have to live with the knowledge that this is what God prepared for you. As we often say, God gave us a cross to carry. He knows what size, what length, what weight is good enough for us. In the end, life is how we want to make of it.

Just like my old friend, Simon. He is the best wine. And I'm glad it didn't take me a lifetime to find him.

It was the best of times—that year. I remember it like it was yesterday. My friends and I were at the launchpad of our lives, about to embark on a life adventure on our own and the entire world was our destination. We were all looking forward to the enchantment and splendor that real life had to offer. We only dreamed about it, but since we were all finished with high school, we were determined to make something of ourselves. There was a lot in store for us, hopefully sweet memories but we knew bitter ones were to come, too, just like drinking wine. Nonetheless, we were all raring to go at it.

Just out of high school and at life's crossroads—my friends and I would not have traded that moment for anything. And brief as that moment may have been, I imagined that it was like a poet that captures and transforms into lovely sonnets that perfect, albeit swift moment when the sun embraces the passing rainbow and sees its colors sweep everywhere. We all felt the throbbing freedom in the air. The thought of finally being done with high school truly lifted the load off our shoulders. It was almost unnerving.

My parents have always made me out to be a lawyer. Either a Perry Mason or a Dick Tracy—they didn't really mind which one. The country's top state university begged for me. They expected me to be another Cayetano Arellano, the first Filipino Chief Justice of the Supreme Court. I personally hadn't really thought much about it. Being a college student was next, yes. But I still wanted to enjoy being a high school graduate first. Those were my thoughts as my pocket already bulged of my college tuition fee. Not really certain of where I was headed, I did make sure that my money was safe from pickpockets. My future career, whatever it might be, was still there and I didn't want any thief stealing it away.

I may not have known for certain what my future was going to be then, but I do believe that I got lost along the way. You see, weeks before graduation, a group of dignified-looking men came during our career orientation. They talked about their work but I wasn't really paying much attention, because as soon as they stood there in front of the stage, I saw Dick Tracy talking about his many adventures. Never mind that these were regular men talking about ordinary careers. For me, they were heroes and I wanted to be like them.

Still uncertain if I was going to be a lawyer that my parents dreamed about, the dean of the College of Law assured me that a law career was still possible whatever course I decide to take. But what my *Nanay* didn't know was that I wasn't even headed to the university. I took a bus that brought me to one of the blighted districts of Sta. Cruz. I think it was more part of Quiapo already, I wasn't even sure. All I knew was that a new school had just opened there and it promised to train policemen and other officers-of-law.

I felt so guilty but I still stepped inside. I could already hear *Nanay* throwing a fit. I knew she would not approve of what I was doing. In my head, I already heard her saying that my first step towards a career in law enforcement was already a violation of the law. *Her* law, that is. Yet I was still determined. I couldn't shake off the idea of searching for truth and justice. I just had to tell myself, *"Hindi na bale, titiisin ko nalang ang mura ni Nanay. Ito naman kasi talaga ang gusto ko."*

While my thoughts wavered between *Nanay's* rage and my dream career, I bumped into Miguel, a high school friend who was also in line for an admission card. We were close friends during our freshman year but eventually, we drifted apart as I was moved to the honors section of our batch. I think he stayed in the same section… I wasn't too sure because Class '55 had 36 sections!

My early college years were made up of general courses that were all possible pre-law classes… you know, just in case I'd change my mind as *Nanay* hoped day in and day out. The only addition to my Criminology major was that our physical education was more intense. We did judo, arnis, and boxing—skills we needed for our future police work. Likewise, the skills served as handy self-defense during the rest of our campus life at the college.

That was my first taste of the wine of life—aah, campus life was sweet, dry, bitter, and oftentimes, stale. Too bland for my own taste, sometimes, until I met Simon.

Simon was a few years my senior. I looked up to him and respected him. After all, he was the one who taught me about the baptism to the world of manhood. We hung out a lot, chatting endlessly about life and love. But he never talked about himself.

In our group of five, I was the only full-time student. Miguel and Cris had odd jobs on the side to earn money for their *baon*. Miguel, for example, braved the big crowds at the Church of the Nazarene, selling *palaspas* during Holy Week. Cris, on the other hand, would be among the many hawkers plying the bleachers during big games at the Dome. Jose and Simon had more conventional jobs. Jose worked for a Chinese trading firm as a *kargador* of their delivery truck. But it was Simon who seemed to have the most glamorous job of all. He worked as a sales consultant for the Philippine Free Press— a hard-hitting no-nonsense news magazine during our time. It was this publication that was believed to make or unmake political parties, even presidents. That was how powerful they were. Fortunately, or otherwise, the paper's reputation rubbed off on Simon. He would quote their writers and columnists and reveal known figures that frequented their office to get on the good side of editors. It was no surprise then that when martial law was declared, they were the first to be shut down.

During school breaks, Simon would drop by his office to while the time away since it was very close to our campus. In one of our chats, I noticed his expensive-looking watch but said nothing since I was too caught up being hungry and having no money. All I had was my fare for going home. I knew Miguel would have just as much with him. So I chided on Simon if he could treat us to a nearby Chinese restaurant for a plate of noodles. *"Wala akong pera ngayon, Pare,"* he said, trying to worm his way out of our invitation. And then

I remembered his watch. So I tried my luck and said, *"Isanla natin ang relo mo, Pare, sigurado mahal 'yan!"*

"Okay lang, kung tatanggapin," he said without a second thought.

That night, we had a feast. That's how Simon is, always wanting and trying to please people. Sounds like wine in season, doesn't it? I remember a time after college when he invited me to a badminton tournament in his office. Simon is a badminton fanatic and it wasn't only because he was an excellent player. His *Ninong,* who also happened to be the general manager of their paper, was also an avid player. You'll never believe it but his *Ninong* won most of the time. Simon was obviously the better badminton player but he was also another kind of player—a wise one. Simon knew how to play well enough to let his *Ninong* believe he was winning against Simon fair and square. I recall those times when he told me about it over good *merienda.* And there were enough leftovers to bring home for the next day. As you can see, Simon was a generous friend as well.

Simon reported directly to a superior in his office. But like some bosses out there who have efficient and talented subordinates, insecurity and envy sometimes happen to the detriment of the employee. But this didn't happen to Simon. He knew how to manage his bosses in the office. He knew how to create situations where his superiors looked good in the eyes of the general managers even if he was the one who did the work.

I remember one particular incident when the paper was threatened by the formation of a labor union that was very hostile towards the management. It was Simon who pressed his boss to run as one of the officers of the opposing labor union that was in better terms with them. Simon, of course, credited his boss for *his* idea. This was his way of rolling the wine in his tongue.

And then there was the girl from the department store. Simon was in love with her. I am not sure why because she did not impress me at all. She was known to be a tease and a flirt. But you should see the things that Simon did to please her! I also recall a fiesta that she once invited us to. Simon was so excited but little did we know that she had also invited another one of her suitors. It was like a scene from a sappy love story. The girl goaded on both men by looking at one of them while she was in the company of the other. I cringed at every bit of it. Especially when she asked Simon for a glass of water and then asked the other guy to walk with him to get some napkins as well! But my poor friend Simon kept falling for it and these two men looked like idiots scurrying around her and trying to beat each other out. That was one of the rare moments that I thought Simon was a dumb pushover. It was so unlike the Simon that I know. That's why they say love is blind, I suppose.

During that time, it was always the girl that Simon and I talked about. He planned to marry her but it never happened. The girl ended up eloping with the other man. Simon was devastated. And for almost three months after that, I lost track of him. He stopped hanging out with me and when I called to invite him to go somewhere, his colleagues at work always said he was on a client call. I never even got to talk to him.

And then one day, when I least expected it, I saw him. I was getting out of a store and there he was walking by. *"Simon, Simon! Sandali,"* I yelled. He turned around and I could not believe that I saw.

He looked haggard and worn down. He had days worth of stubble and his clothes looked like it hasn't been washed for weeks. His first words to me were, "She called me."

I didn't know what he was talking about at first. But he looked pitiful and I felt sorry for him, whatever it was he was trying to say. And then I found out that the girl was unhappy with the other man. And Simon, heartbroken as he was, offered to take her back. *"Kahit hindi ikaw ang una,"* the girl told him. I cringed at the thought of her again. But more this time at Simon when he told me what he had replied to her. "I don't care. I just want to hold you in my arms."

Do you believe in fate? I am not so certain. But let me tell you, on that day that I bumped into Simon, I believed in it like my life depended on it. That chance encounter must have been providential. I invited him for coffee to try to talk some sense into him. Numerous cups after, I finally had him convinced to think about what I said.

I meant well when I asked him what good was it for him to get the girl back. She is married and in the eyes of the law and the Church, this will bring them no good. The other man can charge him in court. And the Church can excommunicate Simon. Are you willing to pay that price for a moment of pleasure, I asked Simon. He didn't have a ready answer but at least, he promised to give it some thought. That was Simon's bitter taste of life's wine.

It took a long while until I saw Simon again after that. School kept me very busy; I had a thesis to write and my graduation to prepare for. And I did. My life after graduation was a breeze. I visited companies, looking for a job and was quite surprised at how painless it was. With a government exam to my name, I truly achieved my dream of becoming a Dick Tracy. And even *Nanay* was proud of me.

But I soon learned that it was not meant to be. I realized early enough that police work was a thankless job. No matter how honest I wanted to be, the temptations were too rampant that it drained and exhausted me to keep fighting it. The last thing I wanted was a fly-by-night-get-rich-quick scheme. I did not want to be a well-dressed man ready to party but nowhere to go.

Fortunately, while I was still in school, I found my penchant for connecting with people. It was easy and comfortable to be around them and I can quickly bond with just about anyone. So before I knew it, I was lining up for a job in an insurance company to help introduce a new concept of protection plan. Riding a bus on my way home one day, who do you think sat beside me? Fate must be at it because it was none other than Simon again. I noticed a feminine-looking ring on his finger. He kept fiddling at it until I couldn't help but ask whose it was.

"I'm in love," he smiled.

So soon? I thought.

"I went with Cris to pick up his girl and she had a friend with her. She talked and I listened. She had a sweet smile and had a way of lilting her voice at the end of every sentence. *Puntong Bulakenya, Pare.* I couldn't get a word in. She made me feel so comfortable. It was a few weeks after that when I learned she knew of my sad love story. How can you not feel attracted to her? Here I was all hopeless about life and love and she had made me forget it even for a brief moment."

I told him to take it easy. The last thing he needed was a rebound relationship. And I cautioned him, *"Kawawa naman s'ya, Pare, huwag mong paglaruan."*

But Simon told me he was very sure that this girl was the one he will marry. I couldn't argue with that. He had already convinced himself and it was already time for me to get off the bus. I wished him luck and hoped that he had found the new lease in life that he had long looked for. It was like discovering a bottle of vintage wine.

Seeing Simon again reminded me of the time when I worked for an insurance company. I similarly had a friend there who was a *probinsyano* and like most of them, he came to Manila determined to have a better life. I introduced him to Simon and our other friends and we all hit it off quickly. Carding was from Nueva Ecija and since there was a long weekend coming, he invited us to spend some time with his family in the province. And what a great time we had!

Our mornings were spent by the river. We just hung around there and let time pass. We didn't seem to ever get hungry because right by the riverbanks was *singkamas* all ready for our picking. We cavorted like anything and had pictures practically naked swimming in the water.

When we got tired of the river, we would go to the church courtyard in the afternoons and played some basketball. We were the Manila Five wowing the girls of Sta. Rosa. I played forward while Simon was the shooting guard. We played with an energy none of us knew we had. We played the entire game with no substitutes. Even my own 20-foot jump shots were hitting the ring without mercy. That kept our spirits high the entire game. Simon always knew where I was and his passes and assists never failed to make me look good. It was my gun-beating lay-up that won us the game. The other team played well but we were better. And we knew it.

In the evenings, I began to notice Simon slipping out the same hour each night. When I could no longer contain my curiosity, I decided to follow him. He was out there doing nothing but staring out at the moon. *"Pare, ano ba ang ginagawa mo? Para kang sira ulo, ano bang tinitingnan mo sa buwan?"* I could not help but ask.

He smiled at me, *"Alam mo, Pare, bago tayo umalis sa Maynila, nag-usap kami ni Maria na* at exactly nine in the evening, we would look at the moon and nurture our thoughts for each other."

Simon, Simon. My friend Simon was truly a hopeless romantic. Very well, I thought. The moon during those days did indeed possess a certain mystique for lovers. Neil Armstrong had yet to take the mystery of the moon away from us.

That summer, we enjoyed ourselves with some bottles of choice wines. Aah, what a wonderful time it was—to be young and free!

If there was something else that Simon and I shared, it was our love for sports. We both could be the best players and spectators. Tennis was Simon's game and had it not been for an accident, he would probably still be playing today. Simon had the speed of Agassi and the wile of Felicisimo Ampon, the legendary Filipino player who captured the admiration of tennis fanatics of the world when he won the Pan-Pacific World tennis tournament. I, on the other hand, was more the Roger Federer who was always ahead of the game because of the uncanny ability to blend power, finesse, and dexterity—all rarely found in one player.

When Simon and I played together, we imagined our power and stamina combined. And with our skill and strength, we knew we would be ruling the courts.

Or so we thought.

I remember planning to play singles with Simon in the covered courts of the Ateneo University. Unfortunately, all the courts were occupied and there was a long line of players waiting. Two young professionals then approached us and challenged us to a game. Knowing we were going to have to wait for a long time any way, we accepted their invitation. We have never met these two men and had no idea how well they played. When we did some warm-ups, I knew Simon and I were up to a diffcult game. We looked like beginners compared to them. In fact, I heard one of them scoffed at us and said, *"Pabayaan mo na, walang magagawa sa atin 'yan dahil mukhang bagito pa."*

Well, that did it. His remark annoyed me and awakened in me an energy to prove them wrong. *"Halika na, Pare. Kakainin natin ang mga 'yan,"* I told Simon loud enough for them to hear.

I must admit, I was a little nervous during the first game. But as we moved along, I was beginning to feel more confident as I also noticed Simon gaining some dominance over the game. Simon would kill shots coming through the net and would return back lob shots difficult to retrieve. His game lacked power but his placements were so precise that we would catch the other team flatfooted again and again. I was happily playing backup most of the time. Simon was like a man possessed and even went for some shots that I could have easily returned from my spot. His game was inspiring and a crowd was gathering around the court to watch. As expected, it was a difficult match. But we beat them 7-6, 7-6 in the tiebreakers. We went over to the other team and shook hands after the game. The guy who made the savory comment refused to look at us and had his back turned. What a sore loser. But his partner was fair. He was even thankful for the exciting match.

If Simon was excellent in tennis, you should see him play basketball. Because of his height, he used to play point guard and his pinpoint passes were overwhelming. He could swipe balls swiftly because of his uncanny ability to anticipate the other player's movements. But his real genius in basketball was not so much in the hard court, but on the bench. Simon coached a college varsity team that everyone believed had no chance of victory. But in spite of everyone's doubts, the team brought home the trophy. When it came to basketball, he was like the legendary Baby Dalupan.

Badminton, on the other hand, is a different sport altogether. It was like a game designed for Simon. He played like he owned the shuttlecock. His shots were so deceptive that even spectators could not believe where they were coming from. Had badminton been a popular and financially-rewarding career, Simon would have been a professional today.

But his love for all those sports came at an abrupt and unfortunate stop because of a coronary stroke. For whatever it was worth, his only son picked up tennis. But unlike Simon, Perry used power in his game. He was good and there were times that I had the opportunity to team up with him for doubles. I could feel this boy's intensity, passion, and desire for the game. I could have mistaken him for his father. It was like playing with Simon all over again.

And the taste of the good life and good wine goes on.

We were sponsors to each other's weddings. Sophia and I were already engaged when I moved to work for a pharmaceutical company. Things were also going well for Simon. He was, at this time, assistant manager for advertising and their paper shared its profits with them annually. But money was the least of his worries, I recall Simon telling me during that time.

But when Marcos declared Martial Law, Simon had to eat his words.

Many said we should have seen it coming. The country then was a mess. Bombings were ordinary occurrences. Even the *miting de avance* of the opposition party was bombed and in that split second, their leadership was wiped out. The last straw was the ambush of the defense secretary when he was on his way to work. Marcos had to do something before he could lose hold of the whole country. As for me, I was headed to my own office unaware that Martial Law had just been declared. It was like any other morning for me except that the *Manila Times* was not on my table. Maybe the delivery boy was running late on his routes, I thought.

It was late in the afternoon when I heard about it. And when it was finally made known to all of us, businesses just like ours stood still in shock. People walked out of their offices and gathered in the cafeteria to talk. There was expectancy in the air. Those familiar with the Japanese occupation feared the return of long lines in checkpoints, the physical abuse if you miss to bow before the sentry, and the showing of the *cedulas*. But for most, many didn't know how to react to this Martial Law situation. This was a first and who knows, the Filipino soldiers may act worse than their Japanese counterparts. No one knew what to expect.

Only the government television was on air. Everyone was glued to the tube while the press secretary read the details of Martial Law. People were advised to stay home and were reminded not to panic because the government was in control at this time. The communist leadership and the underground groups were not incarcerated in the camps. Their effectiveness had been minimized.

However, there were still reports of troop movements going after the military component of the communist party who were poised to attack Malacañang. They, too, were caught by surprise with the sudden declaration of Martial Law. Camp Crame was like a reunion site for the enemies of Marcos. The opposition, that included anyone who expressed dissatisfaction with the government most especially from the media, were all arrested in the first few hours of the declaration.

Nonetheless, the atmosphere in the camp was upbeat. People joked about the situation and tried to make it as lighthearted as possible. The brave ones were candid enough to express that if sacrifice was needed for the sake of the country, they were all willing to do whatever. But deep down, they all feared for their lives. First in the field of media that was shut down was the *Philippine Free Press*. In one sweep, the fourth estate was gone. And so was the livelihood of Simon.

He was trapped in depression for months. Simon's disheartened mind and spirit took a toll on his health. Without any medical reason, his body temperature would rise and fall during the day. He would be shivering in cold during the middle of the day and feel very warm at night. He would be alright at home and would get himself ready for his new job when his knees would buckle down just as he stepped out of the door. He could not seem to get himself out of the house. I pitied Simon. My happy-go-lucky friend was gone.

I remember visiting him several times to help get him off his feet again. "*Pare,* it's not the end of the world. Your family needs you. No matter how difficult it may seem right now, there will always be tomorrow. You just have to fight, *Pare*. If not for yourself, for *Mare* and the children," I would plead.

"Easy for you to say," he would tell me bitterly. And I understood.

Our company was in the best position to gain from Martial Law. We were protected by Marcos and have not lost anything to the political situation going on. We were lucky because we were even able to gain control of our competition. Simon told me I was very lucky. And I knew it, too. But I remained silent in my good fortune. The owner of our company was a close friend of Marcos. We were in the best position to take advantage of government contracts that otherwise would have been difficult for any company to get. As a friend of the dictator, we had the passport to go anywhere, even beyond closed doors.

But still, I needed to help Simon. I needed him to begin helping himself. So I told him, "You are right about my company's good fortune, *Pare*. Our company is even stronger now than ever before. But it wasn't entirely because of Martial Law. We are also in an industry that people cannot afford to lose. Unlike the media where people can get by without their favorite columnist, no one can do without medicines. It is a necessary evil. Our company serves the poor more than anyone else. Without us, there will be those who may die without having taken a single pill. The low price of our products gives them the chance to get better. Now, even as we speak, people are dying without seeing a doctor, much less without taking any medication. Take our company out of the scenario and what would people have?"

"I am for the poor just like you, *Pare*," Simon reminded me. I'm glad he was listening to what I said. He continued, "But it is the media that gives people the chance to be heard. Without the media, who will speak for them? The dictator can now do what he pleases and there is nothing you or I or anyone else can do about it. I admit there were times when we went overboard attacking Marcos; you can even say we might have pushed him to declare Martial Law. But short of saying he is right; the fact remains that he wants to perpetuate himself as leader of this country without the blessing of the people."

Simon paused for a while. He apologized for turning intellectual on me but couldn't help but ask if I remember our history lessons back in high school. He refreshed my memories by reminding me of Patrick Henry who took the podium in defense of what he thought the position of the American Senate must be with regards to the demand of the Brits before the war of independence. He said, "They tell us, Sir, that we are weak and unable to cope with so formidable an adversary. But when shall we be stronger, shall it be next week or next year…? Our chains are forged; their clanging may be heard from the plains of Boston. The war is inevitable. Let it come, I repeat, Sir, let it come… our brethren are already in the field, why stand here idle? What is it that you, gentlemen, wish for? What would they have? Is life so dear or peace so sweet as to be purchased at the price of chains and slavery? Forbid it, Almighty God, I know not what course others may take but as for me, give me liberty or give me death."

I sat silent, too stunned with what I just heard. Simon was reverberating with passion only a man in love with freedom can emulate. Silently, I stood up and looked at him straight in the eye, "Do you think you can make the message of Patrick Henry real with you staying in this house and waiting for your early death? Is that how you want to make Patrick Henry alive in your heart?"

We both didn't say anything for awhile. We feared regretting what we may say next to each other. Our friendship had stood the test of time but at this time, it might not be strong enough to hold us together. These were indeed very trying times. We both avoided eye contact when Maria suddenly came into the room.

She looked at us and said, *"O, bakit kayo ganyan? Anong nangyari sa inyo? Para kayong namatayan."* To break the unnerving silence, I asked for some juice to drink before I headed home. We were both not ready to go any further about our discussion. I would see Simon several more times after that, but we never went back to talking about what we discussed that particular afternoon. It was like exchanging glasses of dry, bitter-tasting wine. It was too bitter for both Simon and my taste at that time.

In spite of our very emotional dialogue that time, I did notice that eventually Simon went back to work. He did a lot of odd jobs to earn some money. A bit of work here and there, working only on contract, if only to earn a few bucks. With his professional experience, looking for a job proved difficult. He was marked by the company he came from and other publishers were now wary of hiring people who could be known to oppose the dictator.

Yet to Simon's pleasant surprise, a publishing house that was introducing a new magazine contacted him one day. He was well deep into promoting the magazine when it was proclaimed that his new employer was running for elections under the party of the dictatorship. These pieces of news floored him. Here he was trying so hard to free himself from the reins of the dictator only to learn that pretty soon, he would be working under a person that represented everything anathema to his political beliefs.

Simon became a man caught in a bind. He had to consider his family who depended on him financially. Yet how would he fathom working for a man who did not share his ideologies? It was like trying to make east and west meet although everyone has already said they shall never meet.

It was a Sunday afternoon when I was having my usual cup of coffee in our terrace when Simon came. It was an unexpected visit since I didn't think Simon wanted to see me again especially after our last conversation. But he was smiling and I noticed the lines on his face were now deeper. He aged in the last few weeks since I last saw him. I was back to feeling the same tension where we left off but Simon seemed relaxed.

"*Pare*, I need to consult with you," he began. "You know me more than anyone else—the things close to my heart, the things that annoy me the most, and more than anything else, my thoughts on the political atmosphere of the country. After months of looking, I finally found a good position in a company doing the same job that I used to. My employers treat me well. They think I can create the kind of image they want the magazine to be. I thank God, for once again, he has made me believe in his fairness. This job gave me a chance to get out of my hopelessness and look at the brilliant light that is back in my life again. But now, I don't know what to do. I just learned that my boss is running in the ticket of the dictator. It is against everything that I stand for. Besides, you and I know the votes have been counted even before the people go to the polls. *Ang biruan nga sa* coffeeshops, *pabobotohin kana, gusto mo pang bilangin?*" He laughed at his own remark. It was funny but there was indeed truth to it.

I took a deep breath and thought about what to say to him. "Life is never fair," I reminded him. "Yet no matter how unfair it may seem, in the end there is always a reason for everything. Don't we often wonder why a person dies in the middle of doing something good? Or how a young man at the top of his class will suffer an untimely death in the hands of a competing fraternity? *Pare*, no one said life is fair. When you look at the history of man from the very beginning, you will read stories of unfairness even from the Son of God himself. Let us not look that far though, *Pare*. Let us just go back to Rizal who, more than anyone else, can speak of our history. Remember how in the beginning, our forefathers welcomed the Spanish people and gave them a piece of our land. We gave them the best of what we are—our sincerity and honesty plus the belief that in spite of our differences, we could be one people. And then what? You already know how that part of our history ended. And because of that experience, it has all shaped us. And you carry that history in your ideals and ideology."

Simon knew what I was trying to say to him. But he still wanted answers on how he will reconcile his dilemma. And I was honest enough to tell him that I did not have an answer for him.

I suppose it is the small reasons and decisions we all make every day that can help us in our struggle with bigger dilemmas such as what Simon was going through. The end may not justify the means, but oftentimes we have to make compromises. And that is what life is all about. Little compromises that one must do to achieve what one has started for the day. In the end, no one will fault you, not even God for the choice that you make. He will simply understand.

With grim determination in his voice, Simon told me he will do it. For his wife. For his kids. Even for me.

We hugged before he parted and I thought this was certainly one of those days that God created especially for people like Simon. The dry bitter wine we drank a few months ago was long gone. We were at this time back to drinking vintage wine.

The Teacher interrupted me at this point. I almost forgot where I was.

Besides my friendship with Simon, he wanted to talk to me more about democracy and leadership—the important things that Simon and I also discussed. He pointed out that the democracy that Simon and I spoke of was limited to human material needs which we both erringly expected the government to provide. Whether it is equal or fair to someone, what else was there to expect? It was too difficult to achieve and the world has yet to come up with a kind of government that can do so successfully. One that addresses everyone's concern and a total solution for all—that government only existed in our dreams.

I wasn't sure—did he want me to err because I dream? Or forbid me from dreaming at all?

Reading my thoughts once again, he explained himself carefully. "You misunderstand me, David. Let me elaborate on what I am saying to help you see the hidden nuances of what public government is about. Government is the human attempt to mandate goodness and ensure fairness. Yet there is only one place where goodness is both and that is in the human heart. There is only one place where fairness can be conceptualized and that is in the human mind. There is only one place where love can be experienced truly and that is in the human soul. Remember that the human soul is love. You cannot legislate morality. You cannot pass a law saying 'Love each other' " (Donald Walsch).

The Teacher's voice was beginning to rise. But I still could not fully understand. So I bravely asked, "With all due respect, Sir, we are not looking for an ideal situation but we do look for fairness in the way our leaders lead us. The love you are speaking of, no matter how small it may be, it is what is lacking in our leaders. The concept of government by the people, for the people, and by the people is used more for self-aggrandizement, for the selfish motives of those who lead us."

The Teacher agrees with me. He thinks our society has found it more convenient to circumvent the law than follow it. He said that surely the prohibitions against murder, cheating, and damaging need not be there if people showed more care and interest towards one another. If there were a more conscious effort to follow the dictum, "Do unto others what you want others to do unto you," then this continuous bickering of what is right and wrong will become an issue not even worth discussing.

I also agree with what the Teacher is saying. But surely, he will also agree with me that the only way to lead with compassion is to always think of the dignity of the human being. It is worth thinking about—that every leader should be able to judge the real progress of society by what is good for many, rather than for the few. This should be for all kinds of government.

The Teacher said, "I understand where you might be coming from, David. In your time, the world has already existed for more than 2,000 years after the death of the Master. His life has been dedicated to bringing love, fairness, and goodness from the person who governs us. It has been a long 2,000 years and the work of the Master has barely just begun. This conversation is enlightening but I do not think there is one solution for this. We all just have to make good things happen whenever we can."

He added, "You know, David, I look at you as a leader in your own right. It is not easy to run a university. But the university is the beginning of what must be when you speak of development. You must remember that the principle of economic development is seen at its best in the classroom. It is when you make it real in your daily life where the challenge to do good begins. How we manage our daily life must subordinate itself to good and this begins at the lowest level of society, with oneself."

It was the answer I was looking for from the Teacher. After all, everything that we do here on earth is in preparation for the meeting with our Creator. We need to help everyone see this, especially the leaders.

The Teacher assured me that the Lord has not been remissed of his promise. The Master, his son, died to give us another chance to be with him again. Let us not waste this chance, which is why it is important to lead the way so that others may see that one can be a saint in the ordinariness of daily life. That money and power are not the answers to heaven. When the Teacher said this, I knew that we were a long way from home. With the way people are today, there is very little interest in the rest of humanity. We are more self-centered than ever before and this is what dictates our everyday life decisions. And as long as we all live like this, we all keep falling back. But as the Teacher said, there is a time for everything. And with this thought, he wanted me to finish the rest of my story about Simon.

With all the accolade that I shower on Simon, there is a dent in his armor that I should tell you about. Simon is a gambler and I think he was born one. Jai-Alai was his game, besides poker and everything else in between. His clients in the media seem to have the same enjoyment, their all-time favorite being late nights in the sports complex of Taft Avenue or the casino. He brought me along with him once to watch a big night of Jai-Alai. It was an invitational game with international players matching wits with local Pilotaris.

I give it to Simon. Jai-Alai is exciting except for the minutes you spend waiting for the next game because the betting lines can be very long.

Jai-Alai produced a hybrid game called Pelota where both Simon and I excelled. But this is where the similarity of my interest with Simon ends. I suppose I do not have the same adventurous spirit that he has. Nor do I have these quick wits in calculating the strengths and weaknesses of the players. Simon gets all the small details that count; from what the Pelotaris drink to who exercises regularly, and even who is going out with whom. These nitty-gritty details may mean nothing to us but to the players, their concentration on the game depends on it greatly.

To make the difference more distinct, Simon puts money on his hunches—something that I don't think I can ever do. There were nights when he gets killed. But the bonuses and commissions he earns all directly go to his hobby. Maria never complains about the lack of money though because all of Simon's salary goes straight to his family without fail. And in Simon's vineyard, you will find only the best wines.

I recall my own father talking to me once about friendship. I have never asked him who his best friend was because I never noticed that he had any. But I was curious so I tried to find out once. Asking him turned out to be a big mistake. He called to sit me down and narrated an incident far too hazy for me to actually remember.

He reminded me about the time when *Nanay* and I were desperately looking for someone to loan us an amount to cover the mortgage of our property in Mariveles. Apparently, the banks were about to foreclose and we didn't know where else to get the money. Then he said it was *Tiong Tomas* who saved us. He just came one day and handed us what we needed. I vaguely remember this but *Tatay* said, he sold the only carabao that helped him till their rice field. When you have someone like that, then you have a friend, he told me.

I never forgot what *Tatay* told me that day. And the kind of friendship that Simon and I have has truly passed the test of time. The Martial Law years brought misery only a man of better roots should have to face. The mountains he had to climb seemed endless. Life was full of never-ending battles for Simon and all he could do was hold on and ride with it. And he did, on each of them, one by one embracing the silver lining that he saw. It tore his body and on occasion, sagged his spirit. He lost everything. But not me. I was always there for him with waiting arms. He may not have always come but he knew I was there and more often, that was enough for him to carry on.

I, on the other hand, had the advantage of a stable career when he was picking up the broken pieces of his. I loaned him some money. Against his wishes, of course, but it was necessary so that he can get back on his feet again. And looking back, I now realize that I may not remember the details of the story, but *Tatay's* words never left me. A real friend is there when you are in great need and has nothing to gain from helping you. It is the way Philemon treated Onesimus when St. Paul convinced the runaway slave to come back to his Master, his friend.

Even the Teacher compared my friendship with Simon to that of Jonathan, the son of Saul. In the book of Samuel,

David had just finished talking with Saul, and Jonathan felt a deep affection for David and begun to love him as himself. When they arrived after David had slain the Philistine, the women came out from the cities of Israel to meet King Saul, singing and dancing with timbrels and musical instruments. They were merrily singing this song: "Saul has slain his thousands, and David, his tens of thousands."

From then on, Saul became very distrustful of David. So Jonathan, who liked David very much, told David, "David, my father Saul wants to kill you. Be on your guard tomorrow morning and hide in a secret place. I will go out and keep my father company in the countryside where you are and I will speak to him about you. If I find something, I will let you know."

That morning, Jonathan spoke well of David and said, "Let not the King sin against his servant David, for he has not sinned against you." Fortunately, Saul heeded his son's plea and swore, "As Yahweh lives, he shall not be put to death."

I was flattered and thanked the Teacher for making my friendship with Simon even clearer than I saw it to be. There is no greater need in this world than needing one another in each other's lives. Somehow we are able to enjoy good years and find the most precious bottle of the perfect tasting wine. Life is good, like tasting the best years ever of the wines in Emmaus.

"Yes, David, you are right. Our friend, the Master, has always been a friend and teacher to us. The hours that we have been walking and listening to your words… you must have a wise mentor guiding you yourself," said another disciple.

Well, we share the same Master, I told the disciples. He is the only true Teacher who cares and who leads. He is always present in my life because I have always needed him. And he has continued to shower me with blessings.

And most of all, he has gifted me with more stories about Simon.

CHAPTER VIII

A Married Life in Emmaus

Married Life

My friends, because they are in love, pass with flying colors all obstacles thrown their way. Listen to the lesson the Teacher shares in the pages of this book.

Sige na, David, go ahead. Tell us the rest of the story.

Before I do that, listen to this song. If you listen closely to the words, it will bring you there.

I Don't Know How To Love Him

I don't know how to love him.
What to do, how to move him.
I've been changed,
yes, really changed in these past few days,
when I've seen myself, I seem like someone else.

I don't know how to take this.
I don't see why he moves me.
He's a man, he's just a man.
And I've had so many men before,
in very many ways.
He's just one more.

Should I bring him down?
Should I scream and shout?
Should I speak of love, let my feelings out?

I've never thought I'd come to this.
What's it all about?

Don't you think it's rather funny
I should be in this position?
I'm the one who's always been so calm,
so cool, no lover's fool, running every show.
He scares me so.
I never thought I'd come to this.

What's it all about?
Yet, if he said he loved me,
I'd be lost, I'd be frightened.
I couldn't cope, just couldn't cope.

I'd turn my head. I'd back away.
I wouldn't want to know.
He scares me so.
I want him so.
I love him so.

The crowd's clapping enlightened me and I couldn't wait to continue my story about Simon.

My friend was a true *Manileño* as much as Maria was a true *probinsyana*. If you must know, there lies a world of difference that is often too difficult for us to comprehend. While Simon was outgoing and sure of himself, Maria was shy and a woman of few words. Manileños are sometimes known to be manipulative, quite often out to double-deal. They can also be double faced if need be. On the other hand, *probinsyanas* exude sincerity, loyalty, and consider their word a true bond of honor. As they say, *"Kung kukunin mo ang aking karangalan ay ano pa ang matitira sa akin?"*

Probinsyanas seem to be bound by a culture coming from the high heavens. As Samuel Maitland said in his essays about the state of religion and literature during the dark ages, "Let not any man then believe that the heaven or the stars, or the earth, or in short, any creature whatsoever is to be adored, except God; because he by himself alone, created and arranged them. The heaven indeed is high, the earth great, and the sea immense, the stars are beautiful; but he who made all these things must be greater and more beautiful."

Maria, in all her simplicity, believed and lived that there is an order in things. The rich are to be given more and whatever the poor have of abundance are meant to be taken away. She also believed that although man is equipped by God with certain rights, it is not for anyone to question him in his decisions and actions. God must simply be obeyed. This belief has bound people like Maria for generations, springing forth the idea of fatalism. Unknowingly, it has also chained them to the dark ages.

Maria was also a woman of strength. She defended her principles with passion. Unfortunately, not all of her practices had kept up with the times. Some of them were still from the Spanish domination and not all of them continue to be true today. She particularly still believed in *anitos* or the presence of spirits that heal. And there was such a person in her community whom the spirit supposedly dominated. It was during these times that his healing power was at its height. And Maria was at his service when people flocked to him. She took it upon herself to decide which people were allowed to be prayed over. Whether actual healing was real or imagined, Maria ended up spending more time with the faith healer and less with her children. My wife and I got involved because Simon had already asked us for help. He was having a hard time convincing Maria to spend more time at home. It was while Simon and I were chatting when Maria knocked and addressed my wife, *"Mare, kakausapin mo raw kami sabi ng Pare mo. Tungkol saan ba, Mare?"*

Sophia was caught by surprise. Although she truly wanted to help, she didn't know where to begin. And she knew how zealous Maria was with the healer.

"Upo ka muna, Mare. Simon was just telling us of your commitment with the neighborhood healer. He was just wondering whether we could help dissuade you from being too involved. Simon is afraid the children are missing your care," I interrupted and spoke in behalf of my wife.

Maria was taken aback as well. She was not expecting this inopportune encounter. It was a family matter, why did we know about it? She felt displaced and betrayed.

"Pare, thank you for your concern. I know we are close friends but this is one thing I cannot discuss with you. It is a family matter," she said curtly. There was no way we could discuss the matter any further at that moment. Could we really blame her?

It was finally Simon's mother who came to their family's rescue in the early years of Martial Law. Help came through this wonderful woman in spite of Simon's misgivings and hopelessness. His mother was working abroad and earning in dollars and this alleviated some of Simon's family problems.

His mother's lifestyle approximated the rich and the famous. She stayed in the best hotels and was used to being served first class. She had people who waited for her and whenever she was back home, she expected the same treatment from everybody. She was also shamelessly honest enough to tell Simon that he needed to find someone of the same status. "Don't shortchange yourself," Mommy would often remind him.

On the other hand, Maria felt the bite of her remarks. She felt very offended by her words but kept them to herself because she truly loved Simon. Biting her tongue and keeping her temper intact was the least she could do if only to keep peace in the family. She can bear those words, she thought to herself. Although she prayed that Simon's mother would not ever go beyond that or else she might not be able to handle it.

Mommy stayed with Simon's sister whenever she was in the country and she would naturally have the first choice on the many *pasalubong* that Mommy brought home. Maria noticed this and to make matters worse, Carolina flaunted those selected gifts she appropriated. These were the other things that gnawed at Maria. There were many occasions that she had held back tears so as not to be picked on some more. After all, they still relished in whatever bounty they had left. Yet, like water constantly dripping on a stone, things have limits. Time will come when the stone will finally break. Maria had almost reached her limits but kept it guarded for the sake of Simon. She prayed for the day when they can live without her mother-in-law's handouts.

Finally, Simon's new job gave them the chance to breathe a little—enough to say thank you to Mommy and remind her that she had more personal spending ahead of her so she should begin to keep some for herself. She was not getting any younger and time has a way of getting the best of us sometimes. Although it was really out of pride that Maria refused Mommy's help, they would have to make do even if in reality, Simon's income was still not enough for their family.

There was a certain aura that one could see in Maria. Her humble upbringing gave her a kind of realness that exuded when you connected with her. Even new acquaintances gravitated towards her. Her sincerity was her magnet. In fact, there were times when a friend brought her along to make a pitch for insurance coverage or a piece of property and Maria found it quite easy to get the clients to say yes. Maria was a natural in sales. And soon, she was out on her own.

It was during this time that Simon began to notice the new furniture in the house. There was also more food on the table and the children were this time taking the school bus instead of hitching a ride with a neighbor. "*Mukha yatang tumama ka sa sweepstakes, Maria.* I've been noticing a lot of things we couldn't afford before," Simon finally said.

"*Sinuwerte lang, nakapagdispatsa ako ng lupa,*" Maria said shrugging it off.

"*Kaninong lupa?*" Simon asked.

"*Matagal na akong sumasama kay Mareng Luming, pinapartihan n'ya ako sa* commission."

At last. The added income that Maria was bringing home created an environment of plenty. Even the neighbors started noticing the changes. Their house was this time being repainted and there were new curtains in the window. Simon was back on his feet again and it was Maria who put him there. Even if Maria did not drink, she was able to provide wine on the table. They were learning little by little and starting to enjoy wine of the lesser known variety as of the moment.

But the winds of discontent would not leave them alone. Carolina suddenly died. And Mommy was back home and stayed longer than usual. She was at this time staying with Simon often because of what happened to Carolina. And this made Maria adamant. She could only take so much of her because after all these years, Mommy had still not accepted her as a wife to Simon. And this time Mommy was living with them, so this was more than Maria could handle.

"Simon, I know you want to help Mommy. There are ways you can do that and not have her stay with us. I am sure there are boarding houses that can accommodate her, places that will be to her liking. Our place is humble compared to the things she is used to. We cannot give her the comfort she wants," Maria tried to reason out.

Simon replied, "Try to understand. Mommy is old. She needs family care more than a place to stay. I know it is just a matter of time before she lets go of her piano playing in the hotels. The hotels she works for will want someone younger, someone that can keep up with the language of today's generation. She is practically half blind and just plays the piano tunes from memory. With her discriminating audience, management is bound to let her go."

Simon's plea was to no avail. Maria still wouldn't budge. And this had been what Simon feared. He no longer had a choice. He had to force the decision on his wife. Mommy would have to stay with them although it was a decision he regretted. But a part of him knew that it was the right thing to do.

His relationship with Maria was not the same again after that. It was like forcing someone to drink when that someone abhors the smell of alcohol no matter how small the dose maybe in a bottle of wine.

The tension in the house became unbearable. Maria tried her best to provide comfort as much as she could but Mommy was never pleased. In the evenings, arguments with Simon never ceased. Their love, life, and even children were affected. It already came to the point that the children were about to take sides between their parents and their grandmother. And then came Edna, Simon and Maria's third child, who took a stand and came to the family's rescue.

Edna took on the challenge of caring for her grandmother. She vividly remembered the time when her grandmother brought home a doll from Singapore. Edna still had the doll to preserve this memory of good times with Lola. She also remembered when her grandmother tried teaching her to play the piano. Grandmother always said she was her prodigy.

Edna could play any tune in her head and finger the piano without notes.

No sooner after that, Mommy became bedridden. Edna had to bathe, dress, and feed her. She even took care of cleaning her when she was unable to go to the bathroom by herself. Yes, it was a daunting task but she never complained, not even when she had to care for her in the hospital. Grandmother was at this time too weak to eat. They had to feed her through a tube. The doctors were trying everything to prolong her life. They even had to cut her skin to get into the veins so they could give her the medicine she needed. Talking was this time a struggle, she could barely even look at the person speaking to her. And this was making Edna very sad. In fact, I remember coming over one evening. Simon had to help Mommy remember me. She smiled and cried at the same time when she finally did. I did not know what to do. The last time I saw her, she was playing in one of the big hotels in Manila and she had invited us to listen. She gave us food and drinks on her account. Edna remembered this, too. And when Mommy finally died in Edna's arms, Simon was grief-stricken.

But her death gave Simon and Maria another chance to pick up from where they left off. They were at ease with each other once again and the children could at this time feel the warmth of their love like it used to be. Forgiveness is the final form of love. Wholehearted forgiveness is almost God-like. And that is what Simon and Maria tried to do.

As I recall the memory of my relationship with Simon and Maria, the teaching of the Lord became clear to me. He died on the cross to save us, yet even as he suffered, he had only love for his persecutors. "Forgive them, for they do not know." This to me is the lesson of Jesus' suffering—to gain the forgiveness of the Lord for the sin of Adam and Eve. Jesus' death freed us all from the bondage of our parents' sin.

These memories also showed the kind of vine grower Simon really was. He was one who knew how it was to love and care for his vineyard plantation. And he deserves all the fruits that life has gifted him.

CHAPTER IX

The Beautiful Thoughts in Emmaus

Beautiful Thoughts

When you are a family that cares, you live only with joys and pains, and as your senior moments begin to dawn, the thought that you are cared and loved keeps you going.

$\mathcal{T}$he Teacher was visibly touched by Simon's story of struggle. But he was in awe of Maria's story of ordinariness. Women during the time of Emmaus did not have rights at all. Yet what Maria faced in life was certainly true to most married couples.

The Lord said that when you are married, you are tied to your spouse and there is nothing that should separate you. The Lord even chastised that when push comes to shove and there are differences between parents and the couple, both must choose to leave their parents if need be. Not out of disrespect and ire, but rather as the means to save the sanctity of the marriage. In the eyes of God and man, husband and wife are one and what God has joined together, let no man put asunder.

The Teacher paused to let that thought sink in. Cleopas had wanted to interrupt but the Teacher did not let him. He spoke again, "Wise people ask: What are human beings?"

Almost all of the Old Testament was written by Jews of Hebraic culture and they express the concept of that culture.

And unlike our own culture, they do not distinguish between a person's spiritual soul from the body. Instead, they see man as whole and in speaking of flesh, body, and heart; they refer to various human aspects. Man is called flesh and blood since he is a mortal creature. Man is called soul because each one is a living being. Soul means breath and the Jews readily identified breath with life.

Moreover, they believed that life was in the blood, that spirit meant openness to God. The heart refers to the inner self, not just to feelings, but also to mind and conscience. Very often, we translate the soul as myself, my life, or I.

Different from animals, the human soul receives something from the spirit. It is blessed with the breath of God. Therefore, the spirit of man is both human and God's (*Bible Teaching— From Christian Community Bible, Catholic Pastoral Edition, Number 83, Page 33*).

Simon and Maria, according to the Teacher, is flesh and blood injected with the spirit of the Lord.

I could not believe what I just heard. I knew Simon and Maria were special, but in sharing their stories with him, I have also gained insight of who I am.

I couldn't help but tell the Teacher, "I walk with you today, bringing back the happiness of my youth and the friendships that I thought I had lost and forgotten. And I realize that I am luckier than most because God gave me the gift to rekindle that friendship again before time caught up with me. This gift I also continue to live with is the love of my *Tiang* Regina and the friendship with my cousin Ben. Thank you for this chance to tell you their story."

I can remember the beauty of long ago quite vividly. It was a time when the air was clean, the rivers were filled with life, and clouds hung with tenderness as the rain added to the pristine backdrop of this place where I found the beginnings of friendship. One of which would teach me about life. Tiang Regina and Ben, how could I ever forget?

I will always remember Tiang Regina who woke up the day with the whistle of kettles and the banging of pots and pans. Breakfast would be on the *lamesa* (table) waiting for us each morning. We were always ready for her banquet. We were so young then. We still ate with our hands.

That was the kind of life we had. After preparing the family breakfast, the women headed to the nearby stream in a place called *Tarak*, a river where the beauty of its banks met the long flowing vine of *camote*. The women were there every day to do laundry and wash the dishes. At noon, they gathered together in the bamboo stairs, their hands working on the head in front of them as they picked and searched for those elusive hair lice. It is a beauty to behold.

My *Tatay* used to talk to me about friendship. He always believed that one may know as many people and have as many well-meaning friends, but when put to test, expect to find only one that makes it. That, Tatay said, is your real friend and no one else.

And that was Ben.

It has always been Ben. My good old cousin and I spent every summer together in Mariveles. Even before I could take off my travel clothes, Ben and I would already be grabbing on a *banca* to paddle ourselves to *Tarak*. I remember the big mango tree in the farm that bore the sweetest mangoes. It seemed to wait for me every summer. Only when I arrived from Manila would the mangoes be ready to eat. And until today, I can still hear Ben's *Lolo* remind me to get only what I can consume.

We would have a feast. The mangoes would be our lunch. Naked to the waist, we would bathe in the river. And from a hanging branch, Ben and I would dive competitively. We both did not know what fear was all about. We would both reach the bottom of the river and bring something up to prove that we touched the ground. Time moved fast. We dove and swam across the river several times to while our summer away.

Then we would take a break by the mango tree. And Ben would bring out his *tirador*. We used it to drop the mangoes we were going to eat. Until today, neither of us would admit to ourselves as to who dropped more mangoes. Was Ben a better shooter? Or was it me? That remains a mystery. But we both agree that the mangoes always tasted better when his Lolo brought out the *bagoong* he just made.

Before the sky darkened, we would make sure to have set traps for crabs and shrimps, our favorite was the *curatscha* in Zamboanga. Whatever it was, it certainly tasted delicious! And when we had leftovers, we gave them to Tiang Regina who served it to us for breakfast the next morning.

Ben and I loved our summers together. We both loved life and each other.

And then suddenly, Tatay stopped bringing me to Mariveles. I don't know why. But just like that, there seemed to be more important things to do and to take care of than visiting Ben. For awhile, Ben and I kept in touch. We wrote each other letters. I was lucky; he was a better letter writer than I was. I looked forward to his mail every day just to know what he was up to, how he was spending his summer without me.

And then he stopped writing. I stopped writing, too. I think we outgrew each other. But neither of us would admit to that, of course.

Many years after that, Ben and I saw each other again. He was at this time a Navy captain and I was head of Unilab. The life we loved has been good to us. We both found our places in the sun.

Then I found myself being asked to do a eulogy. It was Dennis, so how could I say no? Dennis was Ben's son whom I helped find a job in Unilab. There were a lot of things to say, but I could barely make a few words. I choked on my words. But in the end, I knew that I made enough memories with Ben to live by. The stories of friendship that we nurtured in our youth are wonderful tales to pass on to our children.

At the interment, Tiang Regina was crying. She was lost in her thoughts for his eldest son. She told me something I will never forget, it was simple enough but it meant the world to me. She said, "Thank you for being a friend to Ben."

Yesterday, I saw Tiang Regina again. She was but a memory of what she was years ago. Her eyes still twinkled and she had that same smile on her face, but nowadays, you just have to look for it harder. After all, it was a painful afternoon. I sat beside her and held her hand. According to her other children, she hasn't said a word in a long time. I asked her why and she responded in a soft voice, almost a whisper, *"Wala na akong sasabihin,"* and went back to her reverie.

It's been a long time but I suppose we deal with the issue of mortality in our own ways. Life is a cycle; the sound of a baby's cry announces the beginning of new life, followed by the vitality of youth, the slow sense of maturing, and then the forgetfulness of not remembering anymore that eventually brings about a sad prelude to the end of life.

In silence and forgetfulness, one can only hope that you raised your children well enough that they will always remember the love you gave them. Still, whether one is living in a home for the aged or managing a life surrounded by family, there will always be that moment of not knowing anymore.

Tiang Regina and Ben. They both completed the cycle of life, exactly like the way the Teacher from Emmaus told me about. Ben is the beginning; Tiang Regina showed the end of life.

Cleopas clapped his hands to show how much he appreciated my tale of youth. "David, we almost have the same experiences when we were young! I tell you, the more I hear of the people and the stories of your life, the more I like you!"

And then he added, "If you have your story of the mango, I have my own, too. It's not really a fruit in essence, but something that has to do about with it, or more precisely, the absence of it. No doubt, you must know the fate that has fallen on a certain fig tree. Saint Matthew wrote about it." *When [Jesus] was going back to the city in the morning, he was hungry. Seeing a fig tree by the road, he went over to it, but found nothing on it except leaves. And he said to it, "May no fruit ever come from you again"* (21:18-19).

This cursing event in its perplexity has been the topic of numerous discussions among scholars and secular groups; cursing was simply out of Jesus' character! Some say he must have already known that this particular fig tree would not really have any more fruit. It was no longer in season. Yet he went to it still looking for some and when failed to find any, he cast his spell.

What did Jesus have to say about this paradox? I was curious. Because Cleopas was right, it was a highly unlikely event. Surely, there must be an explanation to the curse.

Cleopas replied, "You see, our Lord Jesus deemed it wiser not to elaborate on a number of parables he preached. Clearly, he wanted us to use our own discernment in drawing the lessons from some parables. Its impact would then be more lasting and personal." (See Matthew 13:10-16.)

"But let me tell you," Cleopas added, "upon hearing what Jesus did to the poor fig tree, we were also at a loss. After all, he preached about love and compassion. We discussed it among ourselves and came up with this interpretation."

At this time, I was even more curious. What did the disciples come up with as an explanation?

So you may know, a fig tree's fruits only begin to form when its leaves also begin to sprout. And when its leaves fall off, the fruits naturally follow. That is the cycle of its life. This particular fig tree that Jesus saw had leaves despite the fact that there were no figs yet because it wasn't its season. Therefore, there was no reason why the leaves should be there. By the show of its foliage, it was pretending to have fruit. It was telling a lie through the presence of its leaves, just like the Pharisees who paraded their religiosity but whose lives were fruitless in reality. When Jesus cursed this fig tree, he was teaching us a powerful lesson about being hypocrites!

Jesus apparently had another intention.

Early in the morning, as they were walking along, they saw the fig tree withered to its roots. Peter remembered and said to [Jesus], "Rabbi, look! The fig tree that you cursed has withered." Jesus said to them in reply, "Have faith in God. Amen, I say to you, whoever says to this mountain, 'Be lifted up and thrown into the sea,' and does not doubt in his heart but believes that what he says will happen, it shall be done for him" (Mark 11:20-23).

Mark was reminding us that God has the power to create and destroy. But more than that, he was telling us that we, too, can have the power to move mountains if we have the strongest faith. Only believe, he said, and it shall be done!

After a long pause, Cleopas continued: "Do not forget that Jesus told us another parable which Luke (13:6-9) called the

Parable of the Barren Fig Tree. Here, the gardener pleads with the vineyard owner to show patience to the tree which has failed to produce fruit in the last three years. The gardener promised to add more fertilizers and closely cultivate the tree until it becomes productive. Jesus' lesson here is quite clear. The gardener pleaded and prayed for the condemned tree. The gardener had faith in that particular tree. He strongly believed that, when given enough care, it will eventually bear fruit. His faith was backed up with personal effort. Everyone deserves a second chance to be fruitful. Did I mention to you that our God is a God of New Beginnings?"

I was beginning to understand Jesus' deeper intentions in smiting that fig tree. But I had to ask, was it really an apple which the tempter used to entice Eve?

Cleopas thought for a second and said, "Genesis did not identify the forbidden fruit as an apple, much less its red color. Eden, depicted as a lush garden, must have been dominated by the green color with its thick foliage. I imagine that there will be some red there except for a few flowers and small berries."

"An apple because of its right size and its color became the fruit of choice by early painters and artists of your time when they rendered the Fall of Adam and Eve into art. A small red berry just would not do."

"Now why red? You will recall that in both the Old and New Testaments, there were verses which associate red with sin, sex, and moral turpitude. In other words, sin has always been red, scarlet, or crimson. Even until today, it has retained its notorious identity. The classic novel,

The Scarlet Letter is an excellent example. And then there are your red-light districts."

I said "We have enough discussion of the fruits and the trees. I have a more touching story to share."

The teacher motioned everyone to settle down. By then I could feel how much the Teacher was interested in the stories I shared. I cleared my throat, waited for his nod, and slowly began.

I felt the gentle breeze on my face. It was the same wind on my face that reminded me of the time when my wife Sofia would ever so gently wipe the sweat off me when I lay flat on the floor doing my sit-ups. This same breeze would also caress me and put me to ease as I pedaled my bike with my children during our regular Sunday morning trek.

Caleb used to be always ahead of us as we all tried to maneuver between the potholes and rocks that had become the familiar challenge on the winding path of Moonwalk Subdivision in Parañaque. Caleb would never be in any other spot than ahead of everyone. At his early age, I already saw the burning desire in him to always want to lead, to be the first, and to come on top, no matter what.

Luke, our youngest son, was assigned to keep the pace. He did not push too hard but instead, put himself in rhythm with Caleb so we all could keep a steady speed. Sofia and Lara were at the tail-end as I stayed on the side making sure everyone was safe. Our first stop was always the bakery. The taste of Pepsi washed away our burning throats as we gulped the ice cold drink. We chat a while to plan the rest of the trip. The children would plot our next best route. Tropical Hotel in Las Piñas, they said. Sure why not? It was becoming the watering hole of most executives staying in the village. Breakfast at the hotel was enough motivation for the kids to hang on to their bikes. Sofia would try to discourage us, it was too expensive, she'd say. I would still insist. After all, these mornings happened so far in between that I would feel guilty for not letting them have it. Besides, the children deserved it after the distance they biked!

And then our ride back home would always end up in a race. There was no formal challenge but the competitive spirit had always been a part of our family. It had shaped my children and had been the key in their growing up years. Between Caleb, Lara, and Luke, the race took place very naturally. I would stay back. Sometimes, I biked ahead when the roads became a little bit tricky. And then I'd pull back again when it was safe. Moonwalk at that time was still surrounded by rice fields. From a far distance, the roof of our house would loom. The children's speed heightened as we neared home. And often, Caleb would nose them. Other times, Luke would. Lara would only come first when her brothers were feeling kind and generous.

I reminisce these biking memories with my children often. Especially when we spent vacation days together and then it was time for everyone to go back to work. I would feel loneliness in my stomach. We had just been together on a trip, for example, and then I would already be missing them. I remember this exact feeling when my children left to go to school in California in 1986.

The martial law years changed our lives. We are a close-knit family and the separation was torture to us, especially to Sofia. Only the knowledge that the children were safer there kept her going. Of course, our youngest daughter Timmy made a lot of difference. She was barely five when her siblings left for the university. Her love, affection, and innocence served as the bond that tied us to our kids in America.

Even as new found freedom came after the heels of EDSA '86, the children decided to stay in America for good. They had come to love the place that fate gifted them with. We were lucky our daughter Lara came back. She thought there was enough opportunity in Manila to work. And fortunately, she found her own place in the sun, in the country where she grew up in. Yet, our longing for our sons lingered. As the song says, "You can be friends with your son but you have to be a father to a daughter." And I missed being friends with my sons. America during that time was the place to be when you were young. A bright future was for the taking as long as you put your back on it. And no matter the task, as long as you see the difficulties as challenges and problems as opportunities, you didn't have anything to worry about. This was why my sons made America their home.

Occasionally, Caleb would come home to visit. And while we were thankful for his presence, it is this same presence that makes our hearts long for Luke. His absence was a void, a chasm oftentimes too difficult to bridge. But life must go on. We eventually learned to strengthen our relationship through chatting on the phone and through the internet. Yet it still fell short to touching and hugging each other.

Technology provided us a means to notice the small changes that took place in each other's lives. The noticeable loss of weight or more worrisome gaining too much of it, the wrinkle that begins to cut across the forehead, the thinning hair, the worry we cannot hide because of something that might have happened. We were not there physically to lend a hand; still, we did what we could for each other.

Here we are today, altogether again as one family and now there are sixteen of us. It was Luke's eldest son's first communion that brought us all together again. And, of course, it also included the grand celebration of Caleb's eldest walking up the stage to give his speech as Salutatorian of his batch. These were events we will never miss, no matter how many thousands of miles were between us on regular days. These are stages in the cycle of life which started with Sofia and me. The tree that grew from this seed has gone beyond us. We have begun to harvest the fruits. Good fruits, fruits that will grow more trees of life.

The unfettered pleasure of being together was indescribable. And as expected, it ended too soon. I initially thought I would be bored after being together for a week. I'm a busy man and I'm used to a busy life. Vacation days for me were just weekends. That was long enough. Because in my head, I knew that there were still the never-ending things to do. I want to be always on the go. I was wrong. The realization of the lost hours in the zoo, or playing the bouncing rubber tube in the water, or the endless window shopping in the malls, or the walk on Las Vegas strip, or the golf swings we hit, all these gave me a gush of undiscovered laughter. I had discovered my own children again. And our grandchildren completed the whole picture. The unbridled shrieks of joy and the spontaneity of our reactions belied the reality that most of our life, time and space separated us. We were lost in a relationship we were trying to re-create.

The excitement, anxiety, and fulfillment of a first communion was with the celebrant and with us. Nate made us feel that we, too, were going through our own first communion. As he solemnly approached the altar, we felt the spiritual song that accompanied him deeply. And at that moment when his tongue felt the body of Christ for the first time, we felt the same bread touch our lips. We felt God's presence and prayed that Nate felt him, too.

Nate is a mover in the family and he is just seven years old. Sofia and I felt his pride when he handed us an invitation to his book launch. A series of poems published by his class, Barnes and Noble was the place for showing off their work in public for the first time. I saw myself in Nate's urge to write. The legacy of Tatay who was the first to graduate as Valedictorian in our clan is now continuing on with him. Caleb had also repeated that honor.

Jim, my eldest grandson, is entering the University of Texas with a full scholarship. He wants to major on bio-nuclear medicine. The choice of school is perfect. MD Anderson Medical Center and Baylor Medical University, two of the best medical centers in the world, is right in Texas and this will make him top priority when he furthers his major in hospitals.

Did I tell you yet? A funny story happened on the way to Jim's graduation. My sister, Sarah, drove all the way from

Louisiana to join our family for this important event. She did not have difficulty finding us. A GPS (global positioning satellite) is installed in her car. This thing even talks if you can believe that! Sofia and I rode with her and we were confident that we would reach the auditorium in time. Or so we thought. Because as soon as we started moving out of the hotel, the GPS refused to talk. Not a word. Nothing. It was quiet the whole time. There was some sort of signal that I saw. But wasn't that how it was supposed to be? So I wanted for it to talk. We all just kept waiting for it to say something. *Para kaming hilong-talilong.* By the time we realized it, we were thirty minutes away and going the opposite direction. Thirty minutes in America is like going to the boondocks. The drive to make it to the graduation on time became a struggle. My sister took senseless turns, many times illegal, just so we can make it. Of course, we made it to the auditorium, but missed the best part—the graduation speech.

I felt guilty sitting in the restaurant. When Dinah, Luke's wife, Lara, and Timmy arrived, they, too, had long faces. They got lost as well! With all the twists and turns they made, they finally arrived at the University of Texas. But they were also late. It was a graduation that no one wanted to miss, but we all missed it together.

Another vacation story I remember was when we were in a restaurant and shopping was next on our agenda. Gus, Caleb's youngest, was asking for some spending money. Sophia knew he already had enough but still he wanted more. Sophia insisted he count his money for all to hear. "Wow, that's a lot," she said, sixteen one dollar and one twenty, that's fifty-six!!!!"

We could not contain ourselves; you should hear the howl that greeted her arithmetic. Here she was trying to show Gus who was boss and getting her addition all screwed up!

It was *Tatay* and *Nanay* who set foot in the US thirty years ago. With a dream of a grandiose future, they believed it could only be found in America. That beginning was pioneered by my sister Nina who established the link that became the chain that moved our family to this land of paradox. This is where Christianity blossomed with other faiths yet prayer is not allowed in the classroom, love of country is strong yet the constitution supports the burning of the flag, people died to free the slaves yet never in a country will you find utter violation of human rights against people with just a difference in skin color.

America indeed puzzled us, but this place put food on our table and clothed us. And this is where Tatay and Nanay wanted us to be, where financial progress and search for intellectual might became the definition of our family's success.

It was rare that my siblings and I were able to find the time to be all together once again. We gathered in The Reef, a nice restaurant in Long Beach. It was brunch, that's how the Americans prefer to call it. The whole crowd was there. Our family *barangay* was complete. The reminiscing was endless; the unending flow of faces wanting to meet us, the searching look of grandkids seeing us for the first time, the bussing of cheeks replaced the *mano po* tradition of the past. There were so many stories to tell and to listen to and so many family members to meet. I couldn't all connect the faces to the names that I heard. But I do remember hearing countless endearing words of courtesy that came my way. A nephew said that when you add the family branch that settled in the East Coast, the Midwest, the Desert States, Hawaii, and the Bread Basket of America, we should hit more than a hundred. Our family nucleus was in California.

To paraphrase Alexander the Great, "We came, we saw, we conquered."

America has truly treated my family well. Yet, America is not for me. The blood of Lapu-lapu is in my veins. I imbibe the writings of Rizal and I find the chaos of Manila soothing to my nerves. I want to listen to the laughter of my children, the running of small feet in the grass as my grandchildren run with glee, their innocence I can only envy—but all these, I want happening in Manila.

The Philippine Airlines flight from Los Angeles landed safely. When this family reunion will happen again, I do not know. I hope sooner than later.

I want to liken our family growth spawned by *Tatay* and *Nanay* to an explanation of the story of the true family of Jesus in the Bible (Mt 12:46-50) I found in the book *365 Days with the Lord*:

> Listening to two sweethearts making plans for their evening together.
> He asks: "Where do you want to go tonight, darling?"
> She answers: "I don't really care. As long as we're together, any place is as good as another.

Let's go and watch a basketball game." She knows he loves basketball.

"But," he objects, "you don't like basketball. You said last week you found it boring. Let's go and watch that new movie you said the other day you wanted to see."

She knows he hates movies. He always falls asleep in the middle of a movie. She doesn't want him to sacrifice his evening just so she can enjoy herself. So she objects: "But you hate movies!"

"Oh, it's alright, darling. Anyway," he adds with a smile, "I'll be able to catch up with my sleep."

"No," she says, "It won't be fun if the two of us don't enjoy ourselves together. How about going to a concert of rock music?"

He doesn't go for that kind of music but he wants to please her at all cost. "Would you like it?" he asks.

"Would you like it?" she asks.

And the conversation goes on for quite a while. This is typical of people in love: it tries to unite one's wishes to that of the loved one.

Jesus, the man from Emmaus, knew this perfectly well. That is why he says elsewhere: *"Not everyone who says to me 'Lord, Lord,' will enter the kingdom of heaven, but only the one who does the will of my Father in heaven"* (Matthew 7:21).

It is clear that for Jesus, love is expressed by the union of wills. And in the case of our relationship with him and the Father, this union of wills is expressed in obedience. This does not deny the value of natural family ties; but it does affirm the primacy of spiritual ties in the new community founded by Jesus.

As a consequence of all this, our task as Jesus' brothers and sisters is to streamline our lives with utmost simplicity along the will of our common Father. As my sister Paz would say, "Praise the Lord."

This particular summer may have ended but in the horizon is a new beginning. A new tune is sung even as we recall old songs, once upon a time in a village called Emmaus.

One disciple made a remark. "You have a great family, David, you should make sure the lessons you tell us become part of your family's lives."

"Of course," I replied. "When the kids were growing up, I was supporting them while working for this great company. I was lucky the management was very supportive of the needs of their employees. Many of the lessons I imparted to my children were lessons I learned from our chairman. So, let me tell you about that part of my life."

I spent 34 years in my old company, the memories and thoughts I have are what helped me prosper in my new career. Even though we are retired employees, the company continues to keep in touch with us through a newsletter. There is a writer there who encourages old folks like me to send some anecdotes of the life we had while working for the company. I recall only the beautiful thoughts of my stay and this is what I shared.

Dear Margarita,

Your "Wanted: Margarita" story intrigued me. I hope my story does the same for you.

I am a warrior of Unilab. I continue to be. I am one of those whom they say is an original, a pioneer. Though I am a hybrid, I came by way of stock swap between two leaders in the pharma industry. I may not have started my career in Unilab but I was absorbed early enough to have some claim of being a homegrown warrior.

Ours was a time when streams were crossed by the reliable Unilab Toyota van because most cemented roads did not exist then. Air conditioning was a dream so we all bathed in dust together as a department. We drove a hundred kilometers just to touch base with a doctor in the barrio. *We had to leave the van before a river, ride in a* banca, *and walk for the next two hours to leave our stocks in the only drugstore in town. No, there was no detailing done. The drugstore owner who was also usually the doctor of the town would ask you what was in your bag and the big box on your shoulder. He'd then ask how much the whole thing cost. He always paid in cash and then you had to run and make it to the last* banca *of the day to take you back to the van. The doctor's wife may walk with you a distance while you finish the drink she insisted you take and the rice cake she wrapped for your baon.* "Mag-ingat ka hijo at huwag mong masyadong tagalan ang pagbalik," *she would usually remind you. That was how it was for me.*

As you know, Ambassador Howard Dee, one of the company owners, was very much involved in charity work. In one of his expeditions with some foreign NGOs in the mountains of Banaue, they decided to visit an authentic Ifugao village for whatever help they might be able to extend. The ride in the Land Cruiser could only be so much; they had to ride a horse for a few hours before taking the long walk to the village. Mr. Dee, out of habit, looked for a drugstore first. There was none, of course. That would not be the priority in the village. They have the medicine man who puts together the herbs and concoction to help the sick people in their village. There was a sari-sari store though. They carried a few bottles of San Miguel Beer, some bread, and Pepsi. To his surprise, the store also had a box of Medicol available! Can you believe that? I'd like to think that the pioneers of Unilab made that happen.

The kind of Bayanihan we knew then was the presence that Amo exuded. He was the symbol of trust, someone who looked after us like a father. He was a man whose words bonded us to the assurance that he will care for our family should disaster strike. And he has kept his word and been there when we needed him most. So we worked hard, unmindful of the difficulties, the long hours, the meager pay, and the benefits that were yet to come.

I have kept in touch with Unilab. A few times I was favored with a call from Joy, our new Chair. Those short moments reminded me of Amo's care *for us, of the intensity of a man on fire whose purpose is to serve our country and uplift the well-being of the Filipino no matter how little it may be. Joy has her father's heart. She speaks of her concern:* "Bayanihan, *the soul of the company, must live in everyone's heart. That there be no air that will separate us from each other, the old members of Unilab welcome the new with open arms, the new exert all efforts to imbibe what the* Bayanihan *spirit is all about and in the end, we are all one."*

I am reminded of the reason for this concern. In a page of "Bayanihan: The Many Great Lessons of United Laboratories, Inc.," *I wrote:*

"Even then, the homegrown people in the company resisted newcomers. As such, young as I was and an outsider, the other managers looked at me with cautious disdain. In a way I know how the new generation of people joining our organization today feels, much more so the old-timers. There was a culture unique to us, we who have stayed longest and worked the hardest in the company; we think that we have the franchise to new choice positions that open up. The company will not be where it is today without our personal sacrifices, contented with small salaries, just enough allowances and benefits. We stayed on because of the management's assurances that when the time comes that we will share in the fruits of our labor, we shall have priority to the best portion of the fruit. We looked at the newcomers as usurpers of these opportunities and to rub insult to an already

open wound, they come with the prestige of title, lucrative financial package, better cars, and a parking space to boot.

"The demand for the talents and knowledge that this new employee brings which is not present in the current crop of people is a thinking that is also resisted. Admittedly, the company should have prepared the longer working employees for the future needs of the organization and a strong human resource development program should have been in place. But even if this is so, the dynamic demands of the business will throw the company back since anticipating all the needs for training will deplete the current manpower needed to bring the day-to-day goals to keep the company afloat. It is difficult for a homegrown employee to accept this situation unless one is able to understand and expand his thinking and look at the company's needs."

There is no need to beat a dead horse. Let us move on. Suffice it to say that the company has gone out of its way to recognize the deserving employees while the search for new blood continues.

The day I walked out the gates of Unilab for the last time, I did not feel helpless or fearful of what the future will bring. The umbilical cord was not cut. It was like moving from one house to the next. The Unilab Foundation welcomed me like a long lost son. We think the efforts of the retirees have contributed to the current strength of the company. And in return, the company has shown its gratitude and recognition by bestowing upon *us in spite of our long absence from active work. Once again, I hear Amo saying,* "Pagpasok mo sa Unilab ay lalabas kang Unilab pa rin." *Unilab Forever!*

General Douglas MacArthur, standing before the Filipino nation the day he retired, said, "Old soldiers never die, they just fade away."

It is true, some of us are dead. But we refuse to fade away.

The day I left Unilab, I remember telling myself that I will not fade into nothingness. A new career is waiting for me. The academe gave me fulfillment. You cannot measure the satisfaction of seeing young minds wonder at the discovery of new concepts, new knowledge that you help make them understand.

I was not this confident from the very beginning, of course. I feared the transfer of knowledge. I just took the philosophical nuances of a thesis, but remained unmindful of the morality they project. But young minds are like shoots of bamboo that bend to the wind. I was afraid that with the constant bombardment of unmanaged information for the sake of academic freedom, I will turn the youth into geniuses and experts in their chosen professions, but retarded in their spiritual growth. But I had no reason to fear. That was because the institution I worked for actually cared!

Margarita, you will be glad to know that in between my teaching load and helping manage a university, I found time to publish my third book, The Courage To Be Pinoy: Lessons from my

Father's Heart. *I will be more than glad to gift you a copy with a request that you do a review and hopefully find some space for it in the pages of* Bayanihan *magazine. Would you do that for me, for old times' sake?*

All the best always,
David

And then we were in Disney world.

I didn't think I would ever capture that feeling again. Yet there I was with two of my grandkids. My wife said, "You'll never lose that feeling, the excitement and the awe of remembering the times when Mickey Mouse, Donald Duck, Sleeping Beauty, Cinderella, and all the rest of those lovable characters of Disney were the things that made our day. Seeing them now, I am young again!"

My fondest memories always relate to a marching band. My brothers and sisters tell my friends that I'd drop anything as soon as I hear the sound of a marching band and would follow it all day. Never mind if I left when food was being shared or whether I was doing my homework, nothing could stop me, the marching band was a like dope that pulled me without mercy. And I love it all.

Here at Disney world, no one can beat the sound of the Mickey Mouse Marching Band. With Dopey, Minnie, and all the Disney characters in tow, swinging with the sound only the music of Mickey's marching band can dish out. I came that day not having any anticipation for any kind of excitement. It was just a way of being able to be with my younger son and his family. More than the physical distance that kept us apart, we were victims of an emotional falling out that none of us ever thought will happen. But alas, it did and we were patching up. Being together in Disneyland gave us the chance to rebuild our ties and what better knot could we ask for but the presence of our grandchildren. They were the key to the regeneration of a new beginning, of the life we once shared, looking to an even intense caring for each other.

That youngish feeling stayed with me all day. The Caribbean ride we took, the pirates we fought, and the swashbuckling adventure of being in the middle of a battle between two pirate ships pounding their cannons with all their might, wanting to best the other and be left alone crushing the raging waters of a never-ending sea, gave me back the recklessness of youth. I took it all. Deep inside I felt I may not be able to capture this feeling once more. I don't know if I will still be able to make this trip again. Age is fast catching up and only the feeling I have with my two grandkids, the osmosis of sharing the innocence of their youth is what has kept me going. But who knows, the innocence may no longer be there when we meet again. Time has a way of changing people. The little knowledge we acquire has a way of losing that sense of feeling only our childhood years can nurture. I felt a sense of warmth seeing how my son and his wife lavished us with their love. My son reminded me of memories of us hiking together, biking with the family, and swimming in the pool. That was the time when I still had endless energy and I could swing from work to family and work again with the ease of a flying trapeze performer doing his triple jump and landing safely in the hands of his catcher. Those were my days of invincibility. Time had no meaning and sleep was a nuance you give in to because no one was awake to keep you company.

These beautiful thoughts flooded my mind. They were triggered by the closeness I saw in my son as he related to his kids. They were parent and children, but more than that, they were playmates. They communicated with each other with ease. The kids knew where the playing began and where it ended. They knew when to take their Dad seriously and when to joke.

And the marching band went on. In the flickering of the candle lights, we try to relive our youth. We use all kinds of medication and follow gurus of physical well-being to give us back the strength slowly fading from our grasp. We try hard to hold on. The cosmetic surgeons come to give us a new lift. But it is all physical. What we are looking for is no longer there. No matter how much we reconstruct our body, our organs are tired. The heart begins to murmur, tiring us easily, the lungs wheeze gasping for breath, our pancreas go haywire and diabetes sets in. Which organ will fail next, we can only pray that it will not affect our quality of life too much.

Yet, as the marching band goes, it, too, must end. There will be that moment when the sound of the trumpet, the singing of the clarinet, the swinging of the drums, and the baton of the band leader must cease. Like everything, there is a beginning and an end, birth and death, the alpha and the omega that rules our life. It must show forth its strength.

So I know life will end. How we lived it will be the key to the missing ingredient we are searching for all our lives—to see the Lord and have peace at last, the only kind of peace that my beautiful thoughts in Emmaus can grant me.

CHAPTER X

The Men of Emmaus

Men of Emmaus

*It is a continuing generation these lives of the men of Emmaus.
Their stories will touch your heart, especially that of John.*

At this point, I've already told a number of stories when the Teacher reminded me, "Stories define the kind of man one is. If one's thoughts are clean and without malice, they reflect the kind of heart the storyteller nourishes in him. I once knew of a man innocent in his approach on life. I speak to you of the Master who, I am sure, had influenced you in one way or the other. People followed him without question, willing to die for what he believed in. And these men that became part of his life were simple fishermen and sinners who longed to see the face of the Messiah. He had a special place in his heart for such men. You see, he sought them, knowing they will not refuse him."

> When [Jesus] heard that John had been arrested, he withdrew to Galilee. He left Nazareth and went to live in Capernaum by the sea, in the region of Zebulum and Naphtali. He was walking by the Sea of Galilee, he saw two brothers, Simon who is called Peter, and his brother Andrew, casting a net into the sea, they were fishermen. [Jesus] said to them, "Come after me, and I will make you fishers of men."

At once they left their nets and followed him. He walked along from there and saw two other brothers, James, the son of Zebedee, and his brother John. They were in a boat, with their father Zebedee, mending their nets. He called them, and immediately they left their boat and their father and followed him (Matthew 4:12-13, 18-22).

Philip and Bartholomew, Thomas and Matthew the tax collector; James the son of Alphaeus, and Thaddeus; Simon the Cananean, and Judas Iscariot who betrayed him all did the same (See Matthew 10:3-4).

The better known people that walked, talked, ate, and slept with Jesus were the Apostles. Peter became the first vicar of the Roman Catholic Church, his brother Andrew became head of the Byzantine Church, the Orthodox, John, the disciple became the most loved and, as they say, you know the rest of the story.

"Now David, tell me about the men of your time," the Teacher asked.

My stories pale in comparison with those of the men in the Bible. I knew that and was certain the Teacher knew that as well. But he asked me like it was the most important thing in the world for him. That's how the Teacher is and because of that, I gathered up the courage to recall the stories that I was about to share to him and the crowd that already gathered behind me.

My stories may be of lesser known men than the disciples of Emmaus. Yet in their ordinariness, they have become who they are in my life, almost comparable to your disciples in their own humble ways. And to me they were not any less in their desire to follow the Master.

Let me tell you about one such man I call Mang Piling. He was a barber.

Khalil Gibran, a famous poet, wrote a poem that, to me, describes the kind of dedication Mang Piling had with his craft:

> "Work is love made visible and if you cannot live with love and only with distaste, it is better that you should leave your work and sit at the gate of the temple and take alms of those who work with joy."

Similarly, this seems to be the very essence of what Opus Dei is about; the religious order founded by St. Jose Maria Escriva. It simply teaches that everyone—that includes man, woman, and child, CEOs, government officials, drivers, street sweepers, people from all walks of life—can sanctify themselves in this world exactly where they are. All that is asked of them is to offer their day and their work to the Lord.

In one single statement, this idea levels the playing field. No one is richer or poorer, weaker, or stronger than anyone else. Never is anyone better than someone else. We are what we are in the eyes of the Lord and the best we can do is offer what we have. That is all there is to it and nothing else. God will not distinguish whether the effort comes from a janitor or a manager. All offerings are given equal attention in heaven. The challenge is to improve ourselves in the small things we do day to day.

Mang Piling took this idea to heart. So he worked to become the best barber in town. Even the governor and the mayor were his regular customers. Mang Piling's eldest daughter is now a doctor. The small town looks up to her as well being the best OB-GYN that ever practiced in their area. Almost all the babies delivered in the clinic were her patients. Sometimes, she had ten to fifteen deliveries a day.

Mang Piling's eldest son is a chief engineer in a British petroleum company based in Singapore. His youngest son, now in college, continues to excel in his studies. The boy will soon be given the highest honor by the university.

I remember the time when his daughter enrolled in medicine, their neighbors in the barrio chided Mang Piling, *"Pare, barbero ka lang, ang pamilya ng barbero ay lumilinya sa kapwa barbero. Masyado kang ambisyoso."*

But rather than lose heart, Mang Piling took the mocking of the barrio as a challenge and with prayer, he promised himself with the help of God to carry his children through college. God listened.

A month after his daughter entered medical college, a multinational conglomerate relocated in their town. New customers came and with his fame as a good barber, even the expatriates and managerial staff of the factory trooped to his shop as well. Mang Piling figures that the Americans must be earning a lot because from their tips alone, he got the equivalent of ten heads compared to what he received from his *kababayans*. But more than the earnings and the hefty tips, Mang Piling's satisfaction all came from the faces of his happy customers. In his simple mind, Mang Piling thought of himself as equal to a teacher, the mayor, or even the governor for as long as he did his best in his work. His children likewise embraced the same spirit of Mang Piling towards their own professions.

In spite of technology making the world feel smaller, we continue to still be one of the few countries that can't seem to shake off social class distinction. While democracy and religion may have brought us out of the traditions of the past, our actions and behaviors today belie this truth. We continue to believe that people who are rich and educated belong to a class all their own. The luxury of their environment, their appreciation of the finer things in life, and their taste for food clearly separates them from the middle class but much more so, the poor. Even in the management of our economy, we classify people according to their income levels. Therefore, we have classified society into classes. You are fortunate if you were born to a Class A family. And it's just too bad if you are seen as belonging to the Class E bracket.

What Mang Piling has tried to do in his own way was to break us away from tradition. He was not rich and neither does his family name sound familiar to anyone. But he was proud of his work as a barber and knew he was on top of his game. Is Mang Piling's taste buds educated to appreciate the difference among the best wines in the world? Were his ears skilled enough to know the difference between classical or pop music? Would he have an appreciation for the philosophies of Plato and Socrates?

Well, Mang Piling is a barber. And a barber is a barber is a barber! Certainly no more and no less! So what do you think? Was it wrong for him to work hard so that he can raise children who soon became doctors and engineers?

The answer can be found in Fr. Francis Fernandez's book, *In Conversation with God,* where he writes:

> "All times are good times for entering into the depths of sanctity; all circumstances are opportune for loving God more, for an interior life feeds, as plants do, on the stuff of circumstances in which we are immersed. Growth is the work of the Holy Spirit, plants do not choose the grounds in which they are nourished."

Wherever our station in life is, God gave us the freedom to serve him best. And that choice is ours if we want to pursue it or not. But know that the best way we can exhibit our love for God is in our work. When we love our work, we sanctify everyone around us, our colleagues, our classmates, our neighbors, even that random man on the street. Our life on earth can be measured only with the goodness we have done for our fellowmen. None of the material wealth we have accumulated will matter when our time is here and we finally come face-to-face with the Creator. Even if we are able to bring our most precious possession in heaven, it will pale in comparison to the grandeur that waits us. Nothing material matters in heaven. God only awaits our love as he has done with his own disciples of Emmaus. My friend Mang Piling remains to be a simple man until today. There is no tinge of complexity in him. All he has is pure love for his work and devotion to God.

This soon reminds me of my best friend, Louie. He is the other man with a story to tell like Mang Piling.

I first met Louie as a gangling youth by our company gate. Already right there, I was impressed with his personality which would befit a job in marketing. Louie was one of the many applicants that frequented Unilab on a daily basis. Marketing operations were under my wing so I was always trying to spot a good candidate for the field. I learned much later though that he had decided to be part of the Human Resource group. He was soon assigned to interview incoming employees and this gave him the chance to learn the ins and outs of the organization well. He also had insider information of the most sought-after position in the company—and that was working in the field. That was then when he realized that the heart of the company was in the marketing department, which meant promotions, and which would soon lead to product development.

But I was busy at work so I brushed him out of my mind.

And then our paths crossed once more when his name popped up on my desk one day. He was requesting for a transfer to our department. I hesitated, seeing how he had no field experience at all. The job called for intimate knowledge of the market with a very close relationship with people in the field. My sense told me he would be a failure, seeing how almost everything was stacked up against him. Yet at the same time, his enthusiasm for the work was unnerving. So for that fact alone, I took a leap of faith and signed his papers off.

In the next few months, I heard glowing tales of his adventures and some misadventures. His crazy ideas were moving the products under his care at such unbelievable pace that I couldn't help but keep watch of him. I was always on the lookout for *hotshots* and when you get under my radar, you can bet that you are worth putting on the fast track. And true enough, Louie moved like a shooting star.

But that is not what impressed me. Let me tell you what did.

Louie came from one of the old families of the North. The Donatos ranked well with the Singsons, the Marcoses, and all the old names that gave Northern Luzon its glorious history. Their family was always close to the Lord. They attended daily Mass and, in fact, one of his brothers was a priest. Everyone found Louie easy to get along with. He always made people feel comfortable around him.

But it was his sincerity that caught my attention. He took things the way they were. He listened to ideas and, because of this, had become the master of his game. He did his job as a brand man well. And that in itself is tough enough. Just like in any marketing department, Louie had the responsibilities to make things happen but none of the authority to make them happen. All he had was the task to make the field guys shine in glory and make their product move faster in the market. One could only hope that the "glory guys" had enough compassion in them to realize that it was not their ideas that made things happen but their product managers. Louie was good at this. When he was Product Manager, he was the darling of the field force.

Louie was also very personal when it came to his management style. He thought long and hard before getting into any project. He may not be big with words but he was certainly big with ideas. Change excited him because by nature, he was curious and adventurous. While he welcomed change, he also invested on long-term relationships. Louie worked hard like no other man I have met before, sometimes even more than what the situations called for.

I plucked Louie from his job when my current think-tank guy was ready to move on to bigger responsibilities. As always, Louie went with gusto to this challenge that I offered him.

Modesty aside, I had the reputation of being an achiever in my company. The company newsletter printed a litany of achievements attached to my name. All these were hard earned, of course. But still, I thought it was too much but the Chairman wanted that article published and timed it when he announced my promotion as general manager. Many wondered how I was able to do it. And it was no secret when I told them how. I always surrounded myself with people who were better than me, of course!

Louie was one of my better finds. He was like a diamond in the rough. All he needed was the touch of a diamond master cutter. And that was me. Louie made me look good. He was in charge of properly coordinating the directions of the corporate brands. He did such a wonderful job that we were literally quarterbacking the field force and the Promotions Divisions loved us for it. When we had a problem with one of our joint-venture companies needing to get back on its feet and recover, Louie was there to give them a good push to claim back their rightful share. When I was moved to Business Strategic Planning, Louie was there to get us organized. The company was into an investment-spree and needed to be pointed to the right direction especially in the product categories, and because of Louie, our group became the forerunner of a hard-hitting, intellectually-robust business strategic planning area.

I retired from the company after more than 34 years of service and felt confident that Louie was there to continue the legacy I left in the marketing department. Because of this, I owe Louie a lot. Yes, he is worth his weight in gold. And I'm glad upper management knew it, too.

And now Louie is faced with a new challenge.

The big "C" caught him. Not surprisingly, the attack came while he was helping manage a big conference for his division. And true to himself, Louie accepted the news with candor. Father Joe, the priest to whom we both go for our spiritual direction, said of him, "I am amazed at Louie, he accepted his situation the same way he accepted life as a gift from God. There is no limit to what God can do. All we need is pray and thank him for his help. God knows best."

When I recall Albert Schweitzer's words of wisdom, I think of Louie first:

"The important thing is that we are part of life. We are born of other lives; we possess the capacities to bring still other lives into existence. In the same way, if we look into the microscope we see cell-producing cells. So, nature compels us to organize the fact of mutual dependence, each life necessarily helping the other lives which are linked to it. In every fiber of our being, we bear within ourselves the fact of the solidarity of life. Our recognition of it expands with thought. Seeing its presence in ourselves, we realize how closely we are linked to others of our kind. We might like to stop here but we cannot. Life demands that we see through this solidarity of life which we can in any degree recognize as having some similarity to the life that is in us."

Here is an anecdote that might help you understand further:

God was being interviewed by a young reporter out on his first job. He wanted to make sure his article would create an impact his readers would never forget. For the first time, he learned how difficult it was to choose a person to interview. He considered interviewing the US President, but had second thoughts. The United Nations Secretary-General was another consideration but he thought the better of it. Then an idea struck him. Why not interview God?

Let's give it to this young man how he finally got to the Boss, because if you believe it, there he really was... sitting across God. There were many things they talked about but the young man liked this question the most: "As a parent, what are some of the lessons you want your children to learn?

God gave many profound answers but the one that gave our young reporter the most insight was: "To learn that a rich person is not one who has the most, but is one who needs least."

Louie was never after riches but was always hungry for our friendship. With Louie as my friend, I felt very blessed. And with his wife, Zsa-Zsa, and his two lovely daughters, and God backing him up, how could I lose Louie to cancer just like that?

I had no doubt Louie will come out of this challenge a better person, for he is a true disciple from Emmaus of today.

Saint Jose Escriva said, "An ordinary Christian has to reconcile two aspects of his life that can, at first sight, seem contradictory. There is, on one hand, true poverty which is obvious and tangible and made up of definite things. This poverty should be an expression of faith in God and a sign that the heart is not satisfied with created things and aspires to the Creator; that it wants to be filled with love of God as to be able to give this kind of love to everyone. On the other hand, the ordinary Christian is more, and wants to be with his fellowmen. Therefore, this poverty should be among his fellowmen, sharing their way of life, their joys and their sorrow, working with them, loving the world and all the good things that exist in it, using all created things in order to solve the problems of human life and to establish the kind of spiritual-material environment that will foster personal and social development. Achieving a synthesis between these two aspects to a greater extent is a personal matter. It requires interior life, which will help us assess in every circumstance what God is asking of us."

This is quite a long story on Louie but it is definitely not enough for the real person that he is, I said, looking at the Teacher and my audience.

"David, I know the Lord has only good plans for him," the Teacher assured me, "for our Lord will never cut the life of a good man unless he has other plans for him... more grandeur things, and this I can say with certainty."

I was surprised at what the Teacher said. But I knew that hard as it was for me to truly accept it, he is right. Louie became even more appreciative of life after the best medical minds confirmed their findings. In his mind, he would soon be reunited with God and that was not a bad thing. He did not worry for his family; he knew God will take over caring for them. Which was when I realized that maybe, I shouldn't worry about Louie anymore. He is in better hands with God.

I did not have time to ponder more on Louie because I wanted to make sure that I had enough time to share my story about James, my brother-in-law.

Tatay, may his soul rest in peace, left us a legacy that allowed us to successfully lead a life though not necessarily of luxury, but of comfort. In all his wisdom, he made sure we had formal education, even when there were times we wanted to quit just like some of our more privileged friends did when the going got tough. They left school to enjoy a life of leisure. No more tests, no more reports to write, and chapters to read… but Tatay would not hear of it. We all were made to stay and finish school. The diplomas we eventually brought home were the real treasures of his life.

If bank accounts will be the measure of our family success, we are failures. But if you consider how we have led our lives, we will certainly pass with flying colors. Our family can boast of peaceful albeit ordinary lives. And that has made us champions in the eyes of Tatay.

But true to the saying that in every rule, there is an exception, my sister Sarah, a doctor practicing in Louisiana, got married to a pleasant and exciting, but oftentimes unpredictable, sometimes full of shit man. James made her happy. But he also drove her crazy. Let me relate to you an experience I had with James the last time we were in Las Vegas. I heard a lot about him and how he had been robbing the casinos blind. Apparently, he'd been able to program his handheld computer to predict almost to the dot the winning hand in Black Jack—from the roll of the dice and the number of times royalties have been thrown in a card game, and where exactly that ball will fall in the roulette table.

All gamblers claim to do this and then when the games begin, they all fall flat of their faces when you call their bluff. I put James in that same class of gamblers. All pompous about their skills until they lose a game. But I also have to give it to James because he lives in style. His life could easily be mistaken for the life of the rich and famous. James and my sister have a house in Las Vegas whose living room window overlooks the 6th green of a popular golf course in the city. His two-door Mercedes Benz is safely tucked in his garage while his red Lamborghini sports car remains rarely used because a limo brings my sister wherever she wants to go. Of course, you can't see the speedboat parked at the back of their house. And I've always wondered, what would you need a speedboat for when you live in a desert? But that was James. And to top it all, their mansion is so big; you almost need to flag a taxi to move from their bedroom to the kitchen.

The mansion is magnificent and all the other luxuries they enjoy are almost enviable to many. But don't think it was from James and his handheld computer. My sister has a very lucrative medical career in Louisiana! They have everything, don't they? Actually, I think they don't. Because they've been trying to have a baby for the last twenty years and still no success.

But to James, his Las Vegas was all that matters. When he brought us to Caesar's Palace Hotel, the doorman called him by his first name and asked him which tables he was going to bust that night. When we reached the restaurant, the beautiful hostesses hovered over us and wouldn't stop greeting James because he kept giving out *balato* to anyone who simply said hello.

That dinner with James was an experience I will not forget. We were seated in the best table reserved only for their A-1 patrons and the Captain himself doted on us. The waiters would come running with a slight signal from James. The food was on the house, of course. I couldn't believe it myself until the Captain came to our table apologizing why James had to sign off the dinner still for inventory purposes only.

James doesn't gamble for himself. His clients were the wealthiest from the oil-rich countries and the dot com overnight magnates who fall in line to get his advice. His fee was simple: $1,000.00 upfront and 10% of your winnings. Based on his calculations, his clients win 8 out of 10 times. On very lucky nights, when James's brain is working overtime, his clients make perfect score.

How come the casinos love him when James is breaking their house on those nights? Well, as I told you, his customers are queuing, yet he handles them only one at a time and the rest would have to be on their own for a while. This is where the casinos make their killing. So why shouldn't they fall in love with James when they are able to recover whatever losses they have on that one client James is entertaining while the rest are losing their shirts?

There's also something else about James that will make you either like him when you are on his side, but hate him for when it is about you. He is a great storyteller, you see. And unless it's about someone else, you should feel safe. On many occasions while speeding on the highway, the police radar would hit James. But every time this happens, the officer would end up giving back his license with an apology. The computer in the police car would always signal that the license he has just confiscated belongs to a top secret man. And any further access or inquiry is quickly denied. James explained that thirty years ago when he still owned a photographic memory, he worked with a top secret government project which produced the intelligent warplane called the Stealth Bomber. James claims the concept of that plane was his brainchild. Do you believe that? I don't, that's for sure.

But in spite of it all, I still like James. He makes me laugh. He's the kind of guy I want to be but could not. When I sleep at night and dream, I see myself like him twirling the world in my fingers.

In the book, *Man's Search for Meaning* the writer, a Jewish survivor of the holocaust, spoke of how his mind was able to conquer all the difficulties, the horror, the pain, the imprisonment in a concentration camp, where people were gassed to death for simply being part of a culture that belong to a race accused of killing the Savior. They were the convenient excuse of a mad man who placed the blame of the economic difficulties of Germany to the Jews.

The author found a way to conquer his fears by thinking only of the beautiful things he used to have when life was still a blessing, of the family that loved him, and of the passion he had for his work. He converted the place that was hell into purgatory and made his co-inmates believe that life was not the constant smell of flesh burning, of the food that was not there, of the coldness of winter that bit into their skins, nor the bullets that tore their lives away. When that cold steel bullet penetrates your already almost lifeless form, it becomes like rain saving you from a heat wave that only summer can bring. What a relief, at last, to be free of your mortal pains.

I see my brother-in-law James as one who has clothed himself into the story of Cinderella who allows his imagination to run wild, to look at life with red-colored glasses, to wash away the pessimism of the world because he is secure of himself. But James has always been smart enough to know when to pull back, to recognize the line that bordered between sanity and insanity. He knew that too much sanity would be insanity itself. Therefore, he is satisfied and content for what he is. In his world, whatever he has made of it, he is the king.

How much better life would be if there were more James in the world? It's like having more disciples from Emmaus?

This brings me to the story of my friend, John.

In my earlier book, *Memories To Remember—Class of 1955*, I devoted a whole chapter about my high school friend, John. My narrative revolved around our senior year at Arellano High School where a lot of firsts marked the closing stages of our adolescence.

There were four: first crush; first meaningful but furtive glances at the apple of our eyes; first love note, actually meant to be a shaft of a young heart light, and, of course, the first but clumsy kiss—more of an eyewink than a peck on the cheek.

The less fortunate ones would experience their first heartbreak. It was the end of their world, they would lament. Or so they thought at that time. Years later during a class reunion, they met their erstwhile heartbreakers again. And they silently thanked God for that first heartbreak after having duly noted how differently their former love object presently looked. Or is love really that blind?!

My chapter on John also all too well touched on his early adolescence. I would come to know later that there was much more color, melodrama if you will, in his growing up years without a father.

He told me:

My *Nanay* informed me that my father left us when I was two years old. I was seven then and in Grade One when I found out the real story. I asked her about my father only when I felt left out during our first day in school. Our teacher asked us to introduce ourselves, name our parents, and identify which line of work our fathers were engaged in. Until today, I can still hear the mocking laughter of my classmates when I told them that I did not have a father…

During recess time that day, some of my classmates continued to taunt me and kept shouting, *"Walang tatay, walang tatay. Behhh!"*

This mischievous taunting, albeit innocently done, affected my persona very negatively. Each time I walked out in the streets, I imagined that everyone I met knew that I was fatherless. As far as I can recall, I met my father only four times.

The first memory I have of my father was when we were on our way back from Iba, Hagonoy. It was just right after my circumcision, my uncle who was married to a local lass, brought me to my father's place in the nearby town of Sta. Ana. For whatever reason why they brought me there, I no longer remember. But I remember arriving at this rather imposing house. It looked like a castle to me. His first words to me were, *"Siya ba ang bata?"*

Then we ate lunch together. I took note of our very close likeness and imagined that it was how I was going to look when I get older. During my time, our rite of passage was performed in the most unlikely place. The operating room often meant a nice quiet and shady spot under a mango tree. The surgeon was the town *albularyo* (herb doctor). If he was unavailable, believe it or not, sometimes, it was the municipal fireman! The surgical equipments consisted of a straight razor, usually a Gillette shaving blade, plus any available heavy item which served as the hammer. The patient was required to chew on the young sprouts of guava leaves. He would be asked to spit out the resulting mush on to his fresh wound. This was supposed to be the antibiotic. But, alas, due to the excitement of the moment, the spit would almost always miss the target wound completely. And at worse, because of nervousness, the intended poultice is swallowed!

Starting from the time of Moses until the present, the Jews speak of circumcision as having a very profound religious significance. To them, it represents the fulfillment of the Covenant between God and Abraham.

In Genesis 17:9-10: *God said to Abraham: "On your part, you and your descendants after you must keep my covenant throughout the ages. This is my covenant with you and your descendants after you that you must keep: every male among you shall be circumcised."*

There is definitely more to circumcision than mere ritual. Truly we can find in the Bible a multitude of information about a myriad of things including hygiene principles which would not be known to science thousands of years later!

John continued:

A few days after my high school graduation, when my mother quite tearfully announced to me that she could no longer afford my further schooling, I asked her if I could go and visit my father and plead for financial help. I was sixteen then and it was to be my first solo trip to far away Hagonoy in Bulacan. *Nanay* brought me to the Rabbit Bus Terminal. She even requested the bus conductor to see to it that I get off at their Sta. Ana terminal.

I was unaware how my father knew of my forthcoming visit. As I approached the spacious front balcony of his house, he was already seated in a lounge chair. He motioned me to sit across him. He pulled out a bank book from his shirt pocket, practically slammed it on the table, and declared rather harshly, "Here, take a look at the balance of my bank account. Your mother had always thought I had too much money!"

I was tongue-tied, but somehow managed a, *"Baka lang po matulungan ninyo po ako sabi ng Nanay. Salamat na lang po. Aalis na po ako."* (Mother was just hoping you may be able to help me, Sir. But thanks just the same. Sir, I am leaving now.)

I stood up, let myself out of his house, and started for the bus station. It was 12:30 p.m. My father did not even offer me a glass of water during my visit. It took me almost five hours to do the round trip!

Less than a week before *Nanay* passed away, she told me that I should at least renew my acquaintance with my father. About a month after her interment, I called him to arrange for a lunch date. He was at that time a judge and lived in a real mansion in Valle Verde V.

When I asked him to name a restaurant, he mentioned a popular Chinese place along Pasay Road in Makati. I had hoped that he would nominate a much better and more appropriate place. But I momentarily went along with his suggestion. He was already standing in front of the Chinese restaurant when I arrived. When I got off the car, he was visibly surprised. A second earlier he was looking past my Opel Rekord, obviously not expecting me in a chauffeur-driven sedan. I told him I preferred to take my lunch at the nearby Mandarin Hotel. Half shaking his head, all he could say was: *"Mahal doon! Talagang big time ka na!"* (That is an expensive place. Really you have made it!)

My next remark to him was something I've been waiting to tell him for so many years and that day, I finally said it. *"Utang ko sa Nanay ang lahat ng ito!"* (I owe my mother all this!) He was quiet as we drove to the hotel.

The last time I saw my father was indeed the final time. One early afternoon, my secretary told me that I had an incoming call. It was my father's wife. She sadly informed me of his death the other day. And before he expired, he had asked her that I be informed of his death. Out of sheer respect, I joined his funeral entourage.

I was visibly upset at John's story about his father that I couldn't help but tell the Teacher: "How can a father be so un-paternal to an offspring, a firstborn son at that!? I have always assumed all fathers were like my own *Tatay*—so very loving and extremely caring sometimes to a fault. I do not fail to thank and praise the Lord for my own *Tatay*."

The Teacher replied with calmness in his voice, "Your John is fully conscious of his past with which he was able to successfully steer his future destination. He did not fail to acknowledge the valuable contributions of others in his life. He is ever grateful to God for the varied circumstances that came his way. He was able to prove that no one has to be a prisoner of circumstances or environment for long. Most importantly, he looks up to God as his Father. How can he fail?"

"John did not allow himself to be chained to his 'daddyless' past. He realized that no matter how much anybody failed us, no matter how much our childhood and life traumas trip us, God's gentle arms are always there to lift us to another morning, he, who determines the number of stars and calls them by name, feels with us when we suffer. No wonder he can heal us in his own mysterious ways."

"And may I add," I said, "this wonderful poem that perfectly supports your words, written by an inspired Katharine Simler. Her verses quite graphically illustrate how we all have an immensely dependable God. This is what she said about her poem":

Footprints in the Sand

"One night I had a dream,
I dreamed I was walking along the beach
with the Lord

and across the sky flashed scenes from my life.
For each scene, I noticed two sets
of footprints in the sand;
one belonged to me and the other to the Lord.
When the last scene of my life flashed before us,
I looked back at the footprints in the sand,
I noticed, that many times along the path
of my life,
there was only one set of footprints.
I also noticed that it happened at the lowest
and saddest times in my life.
This really bothered me
and I questioned the Lord about it.
'Lord, you said that once I decided to follow you,
you would walk with me all the way.
But I have noticed
that during the most troublesome times
in my life,
there is only one set of footprints.
I don't understand why in times
when I needed you most, you would leave me.'
"The Lord replied,
'My precious, precious child,
I love you and I would never, never leave you.
During your times of trial and suffering,
when you saw only one set of footprints,
it was then that I carried you.' "

The Teacher nods his head and says, "Our God, John's God, is Omnipotent, Omnipresent. He is everywhere, knowing and moving everything. In Psalm 139:7-12, he assures us of God's complete knowledge and care: '*Where can I hide from your spirit? From your presence, where can I flee? If I ascend to the heavens, you are there; if I lie down in Sheol, you are there too. If I fly with the wings dawn and alight beyond the sea, even there your hand will guide me, your right hand hold me fast. If I say, "Surely darkness shall hide me, and night shall be my light"—darkness is not dark for you, and night shines as the day. Darkness and light are but one.*' "

Someone profoundly observed that life is a grindstone that can grind anyone or polish him up. Your hardships, sickness, pain, and tribulation can either be used as a stepping stone or a stumbling block. But because they are God's Word, we should not have any second thoughts. They can only be our stepping stones.

Our God is always faithful to his promises. That is his divine character. In our own business of daily living, we can rest assured of his uncompromising commitments. *"Call to me, and I will answer you,* [says the Lord] (Jer 33:3), *for I am with you always until the end of the age"* (Matthew 28:20).

You can always claim those promises in your trek to your own Emmaus.

And the Teacher looked at me with a smile. And I believed every word he said.

CHAPTER XI

The Firstborn of Emmaus

A Child Is a Gem

Your child is a gem. You find only pleasure guiding them as they grow up. Yet, somewhere in time conflicts plague this loving relationship you built. It is the same loving relationship that makes you endure.

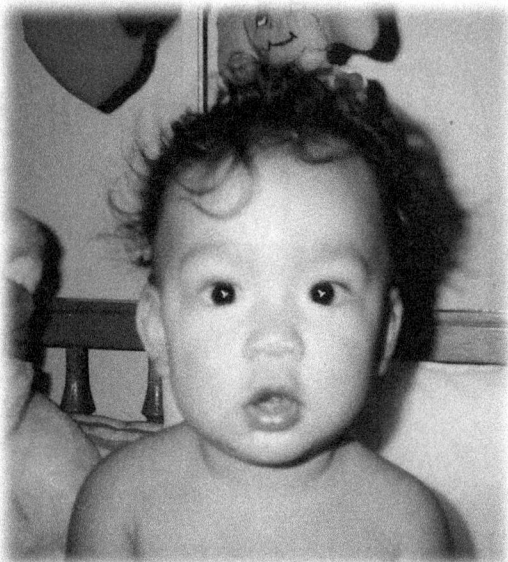

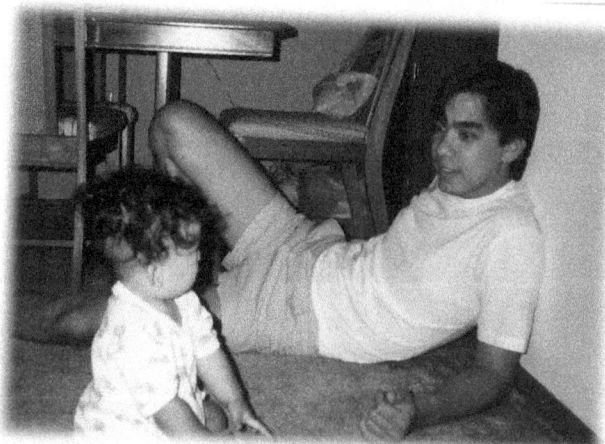

You've mostly heard of stories of my friends. I am glad they have touched you in some ways. Now let me share something more personal. It is about a deeply moving episode in the life of Jim. He's no friend of mine. He is my grandson.

Jim is the son of Caleb, my firstborn. He came at a time when my son and his wife were just about to begin a new life together. They were still unsure of what their future would bring. Jim's baptism, like the presentation of Jesus, was a big family celebration. My three kids had just graduated from the university, pursuing their internship, and preparing themselves for the real demands of the corporate world. Timmy, our youngest, was still in school and living with us. We all flew to America to attend this grandiose event. The ceremony was of the Christian tradition, no turtle doves or pigeons, just Jim receiving the blessing of the Lord during the Holy Mass.

Caleb and his wife were not able to raise Jim yet and needed some time to settle themselves down. So we had the pleasure of bringing Jim back home with us to the Philippines. It was a gift that Caleb granted us—to be able to spend some time with our first and only grandson. My wife, Sophia, loved every minute of it. Our lives changed drastically with Jim around. We felt more energetic and young. My youngest daughter, Timmy, doted on her nephew just like everyone else. He was the first that she ran to when she got home from school. And many times, I would catch her cooing at Jim in the crib before leaving for school in the morning.

Jim loved water. We would spend hours in the club swimming pool until his lips began to shrivel and he would be shivering in the cold. Sometimes at home, we would fill up a drum of water and let him take a dip. Immediately, his head would be underwater and would come up only when he needed air and then down he went again. We enjoyed every minute of the time we had him with us. Everything was fine until he began to have an unstable body temperature at odd hours during the day. We were worried. The doctor said we had to keep him indoors, preferably in an air-conditioned room. His body could not cope with the frequent change of weather, he had difficulty adjusting. We looked at that diagnosis as a blessing in disguise. Even as we have come to love Jim like he was our own son, we also believed that somehow it wasn't enough. He needed to bond with his own mother. So reluctantly, we prepared to return him home to his own parents. Fortunately, Jim didn't seem to mind. He adjusted to his new home and until today, we knew that through God's supreme wisdom, even Jim, as a baby, understood that he must be with his own mother.

We, of course, continued to be visible while he was growing up. We nurtured the closeness we shared and still got the tightest hug from him whenever we visited. In one of our visits, I had this touching experience with him.

"Parting is such sweet sorrow," William Shakespeare said that in a sonnet. A poem he composed for his beloved when he discovered she was betrothed to a prince. He soon found contentment in the separation, for he believed that the girl only deserved happiness like a princess. And only a prince could give her that. Shakespeare was nothing but a Troubadour, a Bard, a weaver of words and of songs, a man not sure of his tomorrows. And so their parting had sweetness in its sorrow.

I was seated in a park in the beautiful city of Bakersfield, an hour's drive from Los Angeles. My wife and I were visiting. She and my daughter-in-law took time out to go to their favorite boutique. I was left to look after my grandson, Jim, who was barely three then. I see him romping around with the other kids his age. Carefree and innocent, their youthful exuberance etched on their faces. I looked at them and saw only pure joy.

Jim lived a life of comfort but the material things that surrounded him did not seem to have made him any different from the other less fortunate children. I saw him reacting like any child when offered a toy or a piece of chocolate. The simplest things easily made him smile. Aah! What an enviable time youth is! Do you realize that the only time we are incapable of judging people is when we are young? To children, there are no rich or poor, black or white, or even pretty or ugly. Their minds are like a camera, capturing only what is and not what we want it to be.

"Lolo, why do you have to go?" my grandson asked me with tears in his eyes. How do you say goodbye to an innocent boy?

It was almost five in the morning when I felt a tug on my sleeve. I was in our room sleeping when a voice startled me.

"Lolo, Lolo, wake up, wake up, Lolo." Maybe Jim needed to go to the bathroom and needed a change. As he pulled my hand with my eyes still closed, I woke up in front of the refrigerator. He was taking out a can of Coke. His little fingers could not lift the tab. It was no bathroom emergency after all! He just wanted a Coke at five in the morning! And then I remembered my daughter-in-law already cautioning me for spoiling this little boy. I thought, isn't that what I was there for? The hard task of discipline was for parents to do, not so much mine.

So we drank some Coke together, making sure that I sat him away from the door just in case his mother would walk in on us. As he was about to sit on my lap, we heard a voice, "Come on, Dad, he should be having milk, not Coke."

My daughter-in-law was serious and she took the soda away. Jim looked at me, pleading with his eyes, "Lolo, please, just a sip before Mom takes away the Coke." But there was nothing I could do. After all, it was my fault.

That's the kind of relationship I had with Jim, we were partners in so many ways. And here we were about to say goodbye. It was sad parting but full of joyful anticipation of our next encounter. So I didn't really end up saying goodbye to Jim. I just made him feel that time and space will have no meaning for us. Technology will bridge our distance. Touch is the only thing we will miss, all else we will make up with the constant hello's over the phone and the internet. But privately inside me, I dreaded the coming days. I feared that, as my grandson got older, his innocence will be replaced with more mature longings. After all, we cannot stop the cycle of life. And I knew that one day, he will have to say goodbye to the innocence of youth. And when he gives his hello to his mature beginnings, I can only hope that the love we shared will stay with him. And even as he steals time for his other priorities, he will still remember the moments we had together. So hellos, goodbyes, and see you later's—they are expressions that can give you joy or sorrow. It really just depends on how you will choose to see it.

Today, Jim is a grown man about to enter college. Somewhere along the way, some seeds of discontent came between him and his dad. The incident became a milestone that changed his life for the better.

Let us hear Jim relate his story:

They call me Jim. We are of Asian stock, proud to be Filipinos. A while back, my grandparents brought their children to America to study. The conditions in our home country were fast deteriorating and a revolution was imminent. The first "People Power" was a creation of the Filipinos. My Lolo David was the proudest of them all. He was in the thick of the confrontation and the final withdrawal of the dictator. Filipinos showed the world how to change governments without firing a shot.

I was conceived before my Dad finished his studies. My Lolo, who expected him to graduate with honors, was disappointed; his expectations collapsed, knowing that his son could easily have brought home the honors which my Dad started when he was still in grade school. He was valedictorian all the way to high school, so it was not impossible for my Lolo to see my Dad graduate Summa cum Laude. It did not happen. I came too early.

But my Lolo is made of sturdy stock. He is an upright man and always in awe of the Lord. He made my Dad make good of his promises to my Mom and supported him all the way until he finished college and beyond.

I grew up in a loving environment. My Dad, a computer genius, brought steadiness to my growing years. He taught me things from good manners and right conduct to succeeding in life and appreciating God's gift to us. My Mom made me feel the tenderness of life. She made my stomach pains go away, including an aching tooth and a bruised knee. I knew I was loved.

I lived in the footsteps of my Dad, not necessarily in his shadow. I did well in my studies. I brought him honor with all the medals I got in school competitions. I was also easy to raise and obeyed my parents diligently. I remember the effort he put in helping me prepare for my eventual entrance into college life. He had such high expectations. He was prepared to send me to Harvard, Princeton, Oxford, or MIT. But I let him down. I only got in a university that fell short of the image of an Ivy League school. All our relatives, both from my Dad's and Mom's sides, and even those from all the way in the Philippines came to my graduation. While no one said anything about me not making it to the Ivy League schools, I knew everyone wanted to ask, "What happened?"

My Mom said I could easily have done it but just that I was too lazy to exert the effort. But she was eventually okay about it and accepted that the university that I would enter was good enough even if it is not as famous as those my Dad wanted me to enter.

I think that was what ignited a spark between me and my Dad—a spark neither of us expected, much less wanted. It invaded our home and never seemed to have left. I remember that in the past, he would let me sleep all I wanted. I could even play all the computer games I wanted even before I ate my breakfast. No one complained or told me what to do because I was bringing home so many honors from school. I never even had to do any household chores. I was spoiled and I knew it. Then the only world that I knew collapsed.

At that time there were rules. I had to live with them and follow them without question. I was also asked to look for a part-time job so that I could learn how to survive in the world, my Dad said. He also told me that I was at that time old enough to assume more responsibilities at home and then had to help both of them. I was also expected to be more cooperative and help around the house, that included helping raise the dog. But I was never a dog lover. In fact, I don't like them at all. And it wasn't even my dog. That dog came at the request of my brother; he should be responsible for him, not me. I hated the dog and resented my Dad for expecting me to walk him and just hang out with him. It took away time from my computer and sleep. He even gave me a curfew on my night out with friends. It was one rule I violated without restraint. I enjoyed my time with my friends tremendously.

Their parents gave them all the leeway they wanted, something my father couldn't seem to understand.

Life in America is very different from the life my father grew up in. In his home country, it was expected that children come home for the Angelus, have dinner together, and then watch a nice TV program right after. My Dad grew up in this environment where family values and togetherness were strong and evident. It was an atmosphere we tried to re-create in our home but it just never reconciled with the kind of family values America practiced. And because of that, it ripped apart my loving relationship with my Dad. It was bound to happen, I guess. In a moment of uncontrolled anger, I threw words at him better not said. He asked me to take them back but I refused. Then my Dad couldn't help himself and started to smack me. I just kept saying, "I won't, I won't," while my tears flowed like water cascading from a collapsed dam.

My Lolo David found out what happened. So he invited me to spend time with them in Manila just to give my Dad and me some space between us. Maybe the separation would make our hearts grow fonder.

They are nice folks, my Lolo and Lola. Lolo David manages a university. He introduced me to a different kind of life. We went to school together where he let me work in the different departments in his school. He did not restrict my movement and I developed some close friendships with some of the students there. We still keep in touch even now that I am back in America. Our day usually ended with a Mass. It was something very different from our lives in the US. My Lolo is able to keep a tight schedule at work and at home and yet have all the time for the Lord. We visited his spiritual director weekly. If there is an experience I will not forget, it is that talk I had with Fr. Joe. He gave me words of understanding and enlightenment. After that first meeting I told my Lolo, "Can I come again next week?" Lolo brought me back to Fr. Joe. He also knew it was good for my spirit and soul. Lolo sacrifices his time with Fr. Joe so I could speak with him. His words are inspiring, it softens my heart and makes me want to go home and hug my Dad and pray for his forgiveness.

My Lolo also took me to a golf clinic. At least once a week, we would play. He had this nice arrangement with my cousin Jose that whenever they played, Jose would take home a good sum, winning from my Lolo. There was no way we would not win. The bet was simple: hit the ball into the fairways and all the shots that do not go haywire gets paid. How could you lose? The challenge was to make as many good shots as you could to bring home more of the dough.

During weekends, we went to the farm. I can still remember when I was younger; I played with the piglets there. That was the first thing I looked for—the pigs. Unfortunately, they were not raising them anymore. They had concentrated on developing the orchards that gave fruits in commercial quantity.

Time with my Lolo and Lola flew. Before I knew it, I was back home and intent in making up with my Dad. But things did not turn out the way I planned it with my Lolo. I tried to talk to my Dad and apologized about the things I said to him, but he brushed me off and said that he was busy with work. I let it go still hoping he would want to talk eventually.

The uneasy peace in our house remained for awhile until that important Sunday night. My parents and I got into an argument about how I'd been breaking curfew again. And this mistake I made became larger and larger until soon we began arguing over the same old things again.

Dad told me that in order for our family to be in harmony, I had to accept and follow everything he said, no matter how much I might disagree with him. No compromises, Dad said.

My Lolo thinks my Dad is right. It is just that he is not able to deliver the message in a way easy for me to understand. He suggested to bring the level of disagreement higher, somewhere at the spiritual level.

The Ten Commandments, my Lolo says, speaks very well of where my position should be in this conflict. Specifically, the Fourth Commandment, says "Honor your father and mother." God did not put any conditions in it. He would have said so if there was any presupposition. The father is in authority; the son is the subordinate and must follow. The son can express disagreement but the father always has the final word. In a way, the father assumes the position that the son maintains respect. But in the end, whether the son likes the decision of the father or not, it stays, my Lolo explained to me.

You see, I don't really understand. Something inside me still makes it difficult for me to accept. It must be pride. Lolo says my parents have the obligation to give me a good future and for as long as I am dependent on them, I must adjust and accept the hard reality that without them, my future is bleak. My Lolo says it is an irony that after I told my Dad those hurting words, I also go and tell him, "Hey Dad, can I have my allowance for this week? I need gasoline money to hang out with my friends. Don't wait for me, I will be late."

Lolo says I should be less intellectual with my relationship with Dad. To be meek and humble and learn to accept the reality that my Dad is my dad no matter how unacceptable things may look from my end. In adjusting, accepting, and doing this, my Dad will not lead me to perdition. He wants only the best things for me, Lolo assured me. Hold back your pride, swallow it if you must, Lolo reminded me.

But no matter how frightful I feel about my life right now, at least I know that my Dad and I are lucky because we are still talking to each other even if all we do is argue. I pray that time will not come when I will no longer want to talk to him and he will feel the same way.

I challenge my Dad's authority, probably way too much and I had to learn to stop. And in all my emotional confusion, there is one person I could turn to and that was my Lolo David. I called him and asked to be clarified on some things I may have misunderstood. And Lolo told me how I am so much like my Dad when he was growing up. This meant my Dad has been there! So I don't get why he doesn't seem to understand me at all.

And then Lolo David said, "Your Dad and I have a great relationship. Just like you, we had our ups and downs when he was growing up. It has not always been perfect, far from it, but he has never challenged me in a disrespectful way like you did. We made sure to keep the relationship of a father and son, respecting each other and always remembering that more than anything; we loved and needed one another. So you must look at things from a wider perspective; the son must always recognize the authority of the father. While the father is obliged to build an environment conducive to a pleasing relationship, the son must go out of his way to make that relationship more than pleasing, delightful if there is such a thing. Do not ever think that you are an accident. You are the fruit of your Dad's and Mom's intense love. Believe me when I say that."

Lolo also said, "Maybe, when you have time, write your Dad and let him know how much you love him. Then maybe he will begin to understand that the perfection he is looking for in you should not be a hindrance to both of you having a more loving relationship with each other."

Lolo's explanations meant a lot to me. Still, my relationship with Dad was eating me, like rust to iron. I didn't know how much more emotional and mental stress I could handle and still focus on college and work… I wasn't sure what to do anymore. And in my darkest moments, I hear the voice of my Lolo reminding me, "Remember Fr. Joe? He has been my spiritual director for so long I do not even remember anymore. He is one person that is very instrumental in the peace I find in myself, the same peace that I share with people around me. I suggest that you pursue your visit with someone like him the soonest you can make in our Opus Dei Center in Dallas. I know they can help you there. The person you want to trust to serve as your counselor should be there. After a while, you can ask your Dad and Mom to also talk to your spiritual adviser, then you would have solved the matter of choosing a referee you all trust."

Then he added, "Today's Gospel reading is from Matthew 11:28-30. *Come to me, all you who labor and are burdened, and I will give you rest. Take my yoke upon you and learn from me, for I am meek and humble of heart; and you will find rest for yourselves. For my yoke is easy, and my burden light.*"

In another talk I had with my Lolo he told me of a nice story:

Johnny was a sturdy robust kid of three. He made friends with a Billy goat next door. Each morning he would pull up some grass and lettuce and take them over for breakfast with Billy. So deep is their friendship that Johnny would spend hours in Billy's pleasant company.

One day it occurred to Johnny that a change of diet would do Billy good. So he went to visit his friend with rhubarb instead of lettuce. Billy nibbled a bit of the rhubarb, decided he didn't want it, and pushed it away. Johnny caught Billy by one of its horns and attempted to get him to eat the rhubarb. This time Billy butted Johnny away, gently at first, but as Johnny grew persistent, he butted him quite firmly that Johnny stumbled and fell with a thump on his backside.

Johnny was so offended by this that he brushed himself off, glared at Billy, and walked away. He never returned. Some days later when his father asked him why he never went over to chat with Billy anymore, Johnny replied, "Because he rejected me."

Lesson: *The surest way to kill a relationship is to insist on having things done your way.*

Let me again share with you another story my Lolo told me to really put my thoughts in proper perspective in my relationship with my Dad:

The English writer, Flynn, wrote about the extraordinary story of Anna, an orphan girl he rescued from the slums of London. And from her, he borrowed some of the deepest insights only the innocence of a young girl can share:

> "If you live in a house and you let the window get splashed and dirty, and you look out that window, it looks like the world is dirty, but it is not. If you look inside the house, it looks like the house is dirty, but it is not because only the window is dirty. All people have two windows. All people have an eye window and then a heart window. The eye window is to look out and see things from. The heart window is to see inside, to see you; when you cry, it is to wash the windows, so that you can see well."

And my Lolo is hoping very hard that I look through my eye window, and that it is clean. I am also praying that my heart window is gazing through my Dad and see only that I am loved no matter what. I prayed so hard, so hard that I cannot remember the last time I ever prayed like that. And indeed, prayer can be powerful. Because one day, my Dad just came to me and said, "Let's go visit this dorm you have selected to stay in." I was shocked because we haven't talked to each other in a long time. And it turned out to be a pleasant trip. He was not happy with the condition of the dorm and asked me to cancel my lease. It cost me $2,000. It's alright though because he brought me along to look at apartments for rent in the vicinity of the school and promised to help me get settled in a better place. I never felt so good. This time my Dad and I are talking again. He didn't even mind my staying late at night with my friends. Everything that happened was a blessing in disguise. I thank God for all his blessings and I made up my mind to tell my Dad and Mom, I would rather stay at home.

Let me now pick up the story from Jim, wishing he remembers the Letter of Saint Paul to the Ephesians, 6:1-4:

> *Children, obey your parents [in the Lord], for this is right. "Honor your father and mother." This is the first commandment with a promise, "that it may go well with you and that you may have a long life on earth." Fathers, do not provoke your children to anger, but bring them up with the training and instruction of the Lord.*

I do not know how their story will end. I do not know where their love has gone. But I will do my best to bring the love they had before. I know both my son and his son are sad for each other right now.

I catch the Teacher intently looking at me. "Teacher, I wish you can say something. I wish it would be something that will help my son and Jim," I pleaded.

They are stuck in between a space so hard to move and get out of, the Teacher said. On one hand, there is Caleb, your son, who must balance his delicate role with Jim, your grandson. Jim is of that peculiar age when he is no longer entitled to the privileges of childhood. However, he does not yet have the complete freedom and self-sufficiency of adulthood either.

On the other hand, Jim demands that his parents give him enough space to enable him to make decisions on his own. At the same time, he fully realizes that he has not yet gained full independence from his parents. He knows he cannot, just now, fully walk out of their relationship and of the resources it brings.

Both Caleb and Jim are now at the crossroads of their relationship and must therefore face up with the difficult challenges. Your son obviously is being extra cautious not to let go completely while your grandson is careful not to sever his conduit to his very lifeline.

I can easily imagine that Caleb took personal offense when Jim wanted to rent his own place near school. He probably felt that he was totally bypassed, even ignored, by his own son in even wanting to live apart from him. Yet, in spite of all of Jim's preparation for his own adulthood, he knows that he still needs his Dad's help. But, of course, no excited child who can't wait to be an adult will admit to that. Saint Luke (15:11-24) wrote about a young son who was just impatient for his complete adulthood. He set out on his own, clearly prematurely, with disastrous results. His good father, who reluctantly stepped back when the son decided to leave, did not completely sever their father-son ties. He joyously welcomed back the prodigal son. He did not renege on his parental responsibility when the son left rather in haste.

Kahlil Gibran in *The Prophet* delivered a profound message to parents:

> You may give them your love but not your thoughts, for they have their own thoughts. You may house their bodies, but not their souls, for their souls dwell in the house of tomorrow, which you cannot visit, not even in your dreams. You may strive to be like them, but seek not to make them like you, for life goes not backwards nor tarries with yesterday. You are the bow from which your children as living arrows are sent forth. The archer sees the mark upon the path of the infinite, and He bends you with His might that His arrows may go swift and far. Let your bending in the archer's hand be for gladness, for even as He loves the arrow that flies, so He loves the bow that is stable.

The Teacher must have read my thoughts. I was thinking to myself, wasn't he being too judgmental of Jim and his contemporaries?

But it was Cleopas who reached for a yellowish piece of paper from his camel hide messenger bag, and said: "Here, read this. It was featured in one of the books of an American author of your time, Sam Levenson. Please try to identify the original writer when you are through reading."

I took the note, and started reading.

> "The children now love luxury. They have bad manners and contempt for authority. They show disrespect for their elders and love to chatter instead of exercise. They no longer rise when elders enter the room. They contradict their parents before company, gobble up dainties at the table, cross their legs and are tyrants over their teachers."

Then I looked up and declared: "This must be from one of the parents in our neighborhood."

Cleopas chuckled with amusement, "If that were the jackpot question in a TV quiz show, you just missed the chance to win the major prize!"

He continued: "The paragraph you just read was actually written by the philosopher Socrates in about late 300 BC! Oh, well. I will leave you now. I hope I have been of help. I pray for peace in Caleb's household."

For a while I sat frozen with my mouth agape. That paragraph could very well been from a 21st century flabbergasted parent. In fact, I recall my own mother saying almost the same thing. Clearly, the temperament of the youth in Socrates' time is practically a clone of the 21st century adolescents. The syllabus of our life follows a uniform pattern: Birth, Infancy, Adolescence, Adulthood, finally Death.

And then the Teacher added, "In his book, the melancholic Qoheleth quite factually underscored our transience (see Ecclesiastes 3:1-8) *There is an appointed time for everything, and a time for every affair under the heavens. A time to be born, and a time to die; a time to plant, and a time to uproot the plant…*"

Someone wrote that the real purpose of trying to open doors for our children is "to build eager, outgoing attitudes toward the demanding and complicated business of living." Caleb, I am quite sure, was not amiss in keeping those doors ajar.

With those final words from the Teacher, I decided that I was going to write my grandson and assure him that things will get better. And I will also write my own son and tell him to open his tight parental hand and trust that he has done well as a parent. And the only way to see how wonderful of a parent he has been is to set his son free and let him fly on his own.

I dedicate this walk of mine in Emmaus for these two men, may they find themselves at peace with each other. I trust the Teacher to find his way through their hearts. He will give me a happy ending, as always, for he has never disappointed me and has always lifted my heart and filled it with joy.

I am sure he will do the same for my son and my son's son.

"The Jew knew instinctively that a good family life must be centered in God and his law. Christians made the presentation a joyful mystery of the rosary because it gave Mary and Joseph joy to present their child to God."

We've seen Mary and Joseph's trust, faith, understanding, patience, love, and respect towards God and, through him, towards one another. Nazareth can teach us about family life in ways that are simple yet full of meaning. We can learn who Jesus really is. We can sense the conditions and circumstances that affected his life on earth, the places, the tenor of the times, the culture, and the religious customs. We can also learn the importance of spiritual discipline for all who wish to follow Jesus and to live by the teaching of the gospel. We learn from the family's silence and, in our time of cacophony of strident protests and conflicting claims, try to appreciate its great value. The silence of Nazareth should teach us how to meditate in peace and quiet, to be open to the voice of God's wisdom. The Holy Family's communion of love and its sacred character can teach us that the formation received at home is irreplaceable (*365 Days with the Lord*).

> *When the days were completed for their purification according to the law of Moses, [Joseph and Mary] took [Jesus] up to Jerusalem to present him to the Lord, just as it is written in the law of the Lord, "Every male that opens the womb shall be consecrated to the Lord," and to offer the sacrifice of "a pair of turtledoves or two young pigeons," in accordance with the dictate in the law of the Lord.*
>
> *Now there was a man in Jerusalem whose name was Simeon. This man was righteous and*

devout, awaiting the consolation of Israel, and the holy Spirit was upon him. It has been revealed to him by the holy Spirit that he should not see death before he had seen the Messiah of the Lord. He came in the Spirit into the temple; and when the parents brought in the child Jesus to perform the custom of the law in regard to him, he took him into his arms and blessed God, saying:

"Now, Master, you may let your servant go in peace, according to your word, for my eyes have seen your salvation, which you prepared in sight of all the peoples, a light for revelation to the Gentiles, and glory for your people Israel" (Luke 2:22-32).

How I wish all firstborns receive their lessons from the family of Emmaus. But just in case they don't, I will carry those lessons with me and pass them on to my family. And from there, I will let the miracle of the Family work its way through, weaving itself to all the other families in the world that have the same faith and love for God.

CHAPTER XII

The Rugged Terrain of Emmaus

The Story of Kuya Is a Lesson by Itself...

In any family, challenges abound. There are hills to climb, mountains to conquer. In the end the family that prays together, stays together. The story is a lesson by itself. The Teacher found silence as the best way to let us learn.

$\mathcal{A}$s we were nearing a group of palm trees, we decided to take another stop. After all, the town of Emmaus is not too far. A short rest will do all of us good. As we were about to sit down, the opportunity to chat came among us once again. It started with learning from Moses, the other Prophets, and the Jewish law. There is a quote from Genesis 49:22-26:

> *Joseph is a wild colt, a wild colt by a spring, a wild ass on a hillside. Harrying and attacking, the archers opposed him; but each one's bow remained stiff, as their arms were unsteady, by the power of the Mighty One of Jacob, because of the Shepherd, the Rock of Israel, the God of your father, who helps you, God Almighty, who blesses you, with the blessing of the heavens above, the blessings of the abyss that crouches below, the blessings of breasts and womb, the blessings of fresh grain and blossoms, the blessings of the everlasting mountains, the delights of the eternal hills. May they rest on the head of Joseph, on the brow of the prince among his brothers.*

The Great Book captures the story of Jacob and his sons; it is the continuing saga of God's love for us. You will find these words in the third part of the book of Genesis, the story of Joseph, son of Jacob, son of Isaac, son of Abraham, and how God tested Abraham's loyalty by asking for the sacrifice of Isaac. Abraham did not hesitate. At the moment when he was about to use the knife to begin the sacrifice to the Lord, God held his hand and promised him that henceforth he shall repay Abraham's loyalty with the covenant that he shall be the head of thousands, millions, and even billions of children, as vast as the stars in heaven, a new nation, one and indivisible.

Before that, God tested Abraham. He was old and could not bear any children. For fear that the promise of the Lord won't be fulfilled, his wife Sarah gave him her slave Hagar and asked Abraham to sleep with her. Ishmael, the son of a slave, was born.

As God's rule dictates, the firstborn is always the anointed and will inherit authority and all the trimmings of power that go with it. God saw it fitting to give Abraham and Sarah a son out of their union, Isaac, the son of free persons, not of a slave. In time Isaac became the father of Esau and Jacob. Esau grew up to have a hairy body and loved to hunt. He exhibited the mettle hunters were made of. On the other hand, Jacob was the opposite. His skin was smooth, his ways gentle, and he would rather spend his time watching his father's flock and dreaming of the rays of the rainbow.

Rebekah, was Isaac's wife was looking for ways to realize God's intention. Isaac, in his old age, had already lost his sight.

So that became part of Sarah's plan. At the point of near death, Isaac was ready to bless his anointed. He called for Esau. But he was in one of his hunts. Rebekah took this as Jacob's chance. She rubbed oil on his body and covered it with sheep's skin to emulate Esau's hairy body. She presented him to his father. Isaac, thinking it was Esau, gave him his blessings.

This would result in the rift between Esau and Jacob. Where love should have been, hatred happened. How can it be when we are all brothers in the eyes of our father?

Thus began the rugged beginnings of the Road to Emmaus.

This last story reminded me so much of my *Kuya*. Without any tinge of envy on my part, I always said that he was the favorite of my parents. And as most firstborn children would, he lived it to the fullest. You see, there are eleven of us, thirteen to be exact including our parents.

We lost our second sibling, Joaquin, during his infancy. One day, according to *Nanay*, he just started to cry and didn't want to stop. No amount of cajoling, wooing, singing the lullaby, or even my mother's milk forced into his mouth could stop his wailing. He cried for days until you could hardly hear his voice and then he just stopped as sudden as he started. But his strength was gone. He passed away before the night was over. My Nanay was distraught. Still crying, she started cleaning the baby and to her horror noticed a missing safety pin that should have been safely tucked in his diaper. My Nanay screamed at the realization that the safety pin must have caused the death of our brother.

Kuya was most loved by *Apo* Juli. She was our *Lola* from my father's side. The relationship of Tatay with Apo Juli was beyond mother and son. Apo Juli was widowed early; it was on Tatay's shoulders that the responsibility to help put food on the table, roof over their heads, and clothes on their back was laid. He was barely seven years old. His brother was three and he also had a newborn sister.

What did a seven-year-old know about raising a family? Nothing. But he did whatever he could. A resourceful boy could find jobs around the *Municipio*, the plaza, the school, and the public market. So every morning, before the break of dawn, Tatay offered his services to mothers who needed help. They give him whatever amount he asked for.

Going to school never crossed his mind until he was thirteen and for the first time, he noticed his mother preparing something for his brother to bring to school to eat. That day, he got out of bed late.

"Are you sick," Apo Juli asked.

"*Hindi po, Nanay*, I just want to rest a little bit."

But his plan was to wait for his brother to go so he could watch him and the other children troop to the only school in their town. That's when he noticed the nice looking girl he had his eye on for a few weeks at that time. She was among the many children on their way to the school.

"*Nanay, ako ba pwede rin mag-aral?*"

Apo Juli didn't say a word. She stood up, took her bandana and left the house. That evening at the dinner table, she said, "The principal said you can go to school tomorrow. Bathe yourself, he said he can smell you a mile way."

Many endearing anecdotes like this made Tatay realize what he would do for his mother. And even when Apo Juli was already dead, Tatay could still hear her teach him how to parent his son. "Be patient with your son," Tatay would hear her say. And I suppose Joaquin's death and Tatay's love affair with Apo Juli sealed Kuya's claim as the favorite son.

Let me move forward and tell you about our family when my Tatay, who learned to educate himself, at that time lived in the small town of Paracale. This place was a gold mine in Camarines Sur, in the Bicol Region. My sister Nina, who came after me, was born there. We completed the children of the first batch—those born during the big war. Our Tatay was some sort of success. He was the number one mechanical engineer of the mine.

Being a hunter, Tatay owned several rifles and his favorite was the Remington rifle. It was every hunter's dream. Kuya and Tatay were close. They both had the uncanny sixth sense; they could read each other's mind. When they used to go on a hunt, Kuya was always a few paces behind Tatay to give him freedom to mark his target and not cause the mark to slip his sight. As soon as the shot was made, Kuya would be running, having anticipated Tatay's line of sight. He never doubted that Tatay would ever miss. It is this kind of confidence one can only find in a relationship built on trust and love. Walking back, Kuya would have their catch on his shoulder. He would walk across town the proudest, even prouder than the hunter himself.

There was this one time when Tatay decided to bring me along. Days before the hunt, I was the recipient of intensive training; I was taught how to be a hound. Kuya showed me the best crouching position to keep out of the target's line of sight, which would notice movements and shoo the prey away. He also tested my nose for different smells. With my eyes blindfolded, he would run items before me, salt, ketchup, fish, and meat, anything that will test my sense of smell if it could tell the difference. He even trained me how to run the forest aware that all kinds of obstacles awaited us. Kuya also taught me how to duck so my eyes will not get caught in the vine with the sharpest thorn.

And the hunt began. I was only five years old. I couldn't sleep the night before. I ran through every tip he taught me over and over so I wouldn't forget. I was ready, I knew I was.

When we got there, I could not believe what I saw. The forest was so lush that the rays of the sun could not get through. It was very eerie. It was the middle of the day yet we were walking in dusk. But I was smart enough to keep this anxiety to myself. Tatay had his rifle ready, cocked, and pointing upward in case we stumble upon a rare opportunity. We were jumping over a rock in a stream when Tatay's foot suddenly slipped and accidentally pulled the rifle's trigger. We were all safe with the rifle pointing upward but we were startled by the thud we heard coming from a nearby tree.

The next thing I remember was running to the spot where the sound came from. Kuya cleared the way for us. As soon as he heard the sound of gunfire, his instincts told him to look at the direction of Tatay's rifle. It was north of northeast. Kuya was already on his way before we could even blink.

To our dismay, we saw a monkey bleeding, gasping for breath, and tightly holding on to her chest, her baby crying. We were all stunned. I don't remember how long we stood there. But it was the monkey's struggle for her last breath that awakened us from our shock. Or maybe it was Kuya's presence of mind that broke our stunned reactions. He was pressing a bunch of leaves on the monkey's chest. He was trying to stop the bleeding but the bullet had hit close to the monkey's heart. Tatay took over so Kuya could look for the monkey's baby.

But the monkey was too fast for us. He disappeared behind the groves, probably fearing for his life. I saw how Kuya's reflexes worked. Every step of the way, he was in the monkey's path not until the baby decided to climb a tree. How could he explain that all he wanted was to care for him, for at that time his mother was gone? We gave up. We couldn't coach the monkey to come down. He was hissing and screaming at us.

Tatay, using his own hands and a knife, was already digging a hole when Kuya and I came back. It was then big enough for the monkey's burial. That was the last time the three of us ever went hunting. And as far as I can remember, Tatay never touched his rifle again.

It was on that day, at five years old that I learned how precious life was—it didn't matter whether it was a life of a human or animal. For all of us are creatures of only one God.

And so our lives moved on.

We were then in the early '50s. The smoke from the Korean War was clearing. The battle was won by General MacArthur in Panmunjom. The Cold War was brewing. The Russians had a strangle hold of Eastern Europe and felt threatened by the nuclear power of America. Escolta was the undisputed business center and girls were in love with the young and dashing Frank Sinatra, and the Platters were number one in Manila. The airwaves were clogged with Joni James' "I'll Be Seeing You" and the Maguire Sisters' "Sincerely." The number one song was "The Sandman." It was also the year that the "Ten Commandments" captured moviegoers by storm.

The film that moved my heart though was "Lily." I remember that song with more sentimentality because it was the first dance my crush granted me. Ah, the thrills of puppy love in spite of the fact that she winced every time I stepped on her dainty feet when we danced.

Would you believe that in high school, I got by with only thirty centavos a day? Today, that barely buys a piece of candy. It may not be worth much for some but to me, they were thirty wonderful centavos that were all mine to use. A jeepney ride to and from school cost twenty centavos and all throughout my ride, I made sure to hold on to all my money. Losing it would mean walking twelve kilometers. If you discover too late that you lost your centavos, you would have to swallow your pride as the driver spit his obscenities at you in front of everyone. The only thing that could take you home from there was bowing your head in shame.

I still remember the Chinese bakery fronting our school. My mornings consisted of a choice between munching on *machacao* (day-old bread recooked that I swear were as hard as stone) or downing a bottle of Cosmos. If I was really hungry, I would go for the *machacao* and the free water the *kabisi* would hand me to help push the bread down my throat. That was where my first five centavos of the day went. The taste of the machacao still lingers in my mouth until today. I have never tasted anything as disgusting but I would gladly eat it all over again if I could. It was that dreadful Chinese bread that taught me an important life lesson—humility. *Kuya* got P20 allowance for the week. Unbelievable as it may seem, he deserved every penny.

The '50s were the years of economic struggle for our family. Tatay was doing what he loved most, working as mechanical engineer in a company designed to help the country get back on its feet. His earnings were enough to put food on the table and send nine children to school. At the end of the day, nothing was left.

He tried hard to offer his services in the barrio as an electrician or an auto mechanic. He even went with construction workers on weekends, hoping for some additional income. Tatay felt he was not providing for us enough. The most that he could do was to stretch himself at work, hoping his boss was watching so to give him a raise or promote him to a higher position. He was a professional. He was good at perfecting his skills, doing a good job, and making other people rich.

Nanay, on the other hand, was the businesswoman, the entrepreneur in our family. She put up a *sari-sari* store and sold items our neighbors needed. She woke up at dawn, visited the market, passed by the bakery and the grocery even before our neighbors were up. Her fish, vegetables, ice, canned goods, and *pandesal* were laid out in the counter for her customers to pick. It went fast, the items were sold before midday and then she would ask one of us to tend her store. It was usually *Ate* Anna. And then Nanay would go back and get more goods. And our family *alkansya* began to fill.

The natural recovery after the devastation of the big war brought forth frenzied reconstruction. Our barrio was the site of a big brewery plant. So the people from our town got to enjoy beer as they relaxed after a hard day's work. The plant was a magnet for transient workers as well. The other magnet was the slaughterhouse. As families settled in and grew because of the employment the beer brewery and the *Matadero* had to offer, housing facilities in our area began to suffer.

It was Nanay's idea that we deal into real estate. This meant putting up more rooms to rent out for the workers who came in droves. The rooms which were supposed to accommodate two or three people became homes for families. My father was the implementer in the partnership. He put up rooms that became flats and did it as fast as the settlers came. The acumen of my mother for business was apparent. She bought pieces of properties surrounding our house and before we knew it, we were the "for-rent kings" in the neighborhood.

Someone had to attend to the maintenance of these rooms. My father was at work during the day. Kuya and I would be in school in the mornings. So before Tatay left for work, he would have a long list of things to do for Kuya who used me as his peon. Kuya became the builder of Marulas.

While most young boys were into basketball, fishing in Tuliahan River, or just simply cavorting with their *barkada*, *Kuya* was deep at work finishing the work Tatay left him. Kuya is a wonder. I do not know where he got his skills; there was nothing complicated or too difficult for him to do. One day he's a carpenter, the next a painter, an electrician, a mason—he was everything Tatay needed to accomplish the things to do in the list. And he never complained. The only thing he made sure I did was to continually supply him with his favorite candy, called *panutsa* which literally meant sweet in a coconut shell.

Many times, Tatay would also leave assignments for me, too. Mine were easy assignments just so I won't feel left out. But I was not built like Kuya. I was a sickly child and always had asthma. The moment Kuya noticed me coughing or breathing deeply, he would come down from the roof, get me a glass of cold water, and take me away from whatever was causing my attack. These were tender moments with him I will never forget. I knew my Kuya loved me.

Before the day was over, Kuya and I would find a comfortable place and we would review the day's list. He was a hard worker, not a slacker. He was also like Tatay, a perfectionist. Even until today, you will still see the vestige of Kuya's work, they lasted all these years because it was work done by an artist.

It was also no wonder that while I leave for school with only thirty centavos in my pocket; Kuya, at times, can get away with twenty pesos and he deserves it.

The Teacher wanted to give more meaning to what I said about the vestige of Kuya's work.

"More than sixty years ago, a man gathered his own father's carpentry tools and single-handedly constructed what could pass as rooms decent enough for anyone to live in. Their family has grown and as a brother or sister gets married, the eldest brother would build shelters to have roof over their heads. Definitely, he is not your usual head carpenter, not even a second-rate *capataz* or construction helper. However, the structures that he built, amateurish and as simple as they were, still stand today!"

"We are reminded of the ark which the saintly Noah built. He did not have the skills of a marine engineer or a professional boat builder. But he was guided by a blueprint provided by Yahweh. His Ark withstood the buffeting of forty days and forty nights of a torrential deluge!"

"In direct contrast, the most brilliant marine engineers, hydrologic experts, and metal craftsmen of their time pooled in their talents to build what was supposed to be an unsinkable ocean vessel. Alas, she sank on her maiden voyage. She was the Titanic."

"In the relatively recent times, there was a carpentry feat which, up to this time, has no logical or satisfactory explanation. It was in December 1878. The almost completed Chapel of Our Lady of Light in Santa Fe had been scheduled to be blessed by the archbishop by early April the following year. Yet, they had one seemingly insurmountable problem. With the intention of building an impressive structure honoring its Patroness, the bishop had earlier commissioned an architect in Paris to draw its plans, this, against the protestations of the mother superior. She was worried that if something went wrong in the building process, where could she go? But the bishop was adamant. The future chapel must look like a smaller version of the Sainte Chappell in Paris. A few minor finishing touches would complete the construction. On the outside the new chapel indeed looked beautiful. The interior was as imposing. The inauguration could have been done as planned, were it not for the momentary absent-mindedness of the French architect. The choir loft was not provided with a means of access unless through a ladder! Worse, there was not enough space on the chapel floor to accommodate the supports and steps a regular staircase needed. Local carpenters and prominent wood craftsmen were summoned. All shook their heads. Impossible!"

"But one of those carpenters kept coming back, asking for a chance to try his hands at the all-important staircase. The first time he presented himself, the mother superior was not the least impressed. She was afraid this man might only spoil the chapel's beautiful interior with his hit-or-miss method. That morning, while the mother superior was busy preparing to leave for the neighboring town, the carpenter was back at the convent house again and wanted to talk to her. At his persistence, she raised her arms in surrender and finally gave him permission. But she sternly warned him not to drive the first nail until he is 100% sure he can build the much coveted staircase. With that, she left."

"The carpenter went to work right away but not before he installed a curtain around the work area so as to prevent his saw dusts from going to the chapel interior. During his brief rest periods, the other nuns noticed that one of the convent's wards clearly enjoyed sitting down in an animated conversation with the carpenter. She was a twelve-year orphan girl adopted by the Sisters. She was also mute. She could hear and understand but the Sisters were unsuccessful in coaching her to talk."

"Each morning, the carpenter used to come in with a load of lumber on his burro. He used to leave before nightfall. This went on until about three weeks later, when the mother superior arrived at the convent's door. Immediately she noticed the interior lamps were all lighted, and sensed a very strong excitement among the other sisters inside. She was immediately led to the vicinity of the choir loft. And lo and behold, a circular staircase rose before them! Its base was on the chapel floor and its top rested on the choir loft. It appeared floating on air!"

"The mother superior gingerly approached the staircase. Tentatively, she set foot on the first step and then the second. There was not the slightest movement. The circular stairs seemed to be anchored securely to the center of the earth! The Sisters informed the Reverend Mother that the carpenter finished the day before. He refused any offer of payment and no one has seen him since."

" 'But who was he?' mother superior asked, 'You did not even ask for his name.' At this, the twelve-year orphan pushed herself forward. She took a very deep breath and uttered a sound which was still undecipherable. The nuns stood transfixed waiting for her attempt at speech. Slowly, the orphan labored with a clear syllable— 'Jo'… followed by a second, '…se.' She was crying now, and repeated the first word she had ever uttered—'Jose.' "

"The nuns crossed themselves. The girl spoke again, this time with great clarity so that there was no mistaking the first name of their mysterious carpenter. 'Jose!' "

"Jose, the Spanish word for Joseph, Joseph the Master Carpenter!"

"It is said that the structure can still be seen today in a chapel in Santa Fe where it was dedicated more than a century ago. Visiting architects and engineers from around the world can only marvel at the ingenuity of the construction. 'Impossible' was all they could mutter. The stairs, all 33-steps, made two complete turns without central support. No nails were used, only wooden pegs. The joints were made in perfect precision. The wood is reported to be of a variety not found in New Mexico. Clearly the number of steps was intentional, representing the number of Jesus' earth years!"

I was amazed at the story. Truly it pales in comparison with what Kuya has built, but the same faith, emotion, and dedication they both had for their craft was clearly similar!

But Kuya's life was not all rosy though. His adventurous spirit led him to a career in maritime engineering. The state academy was located in Pasay, near the famous Dewey Boulevard along Manila Bay. You should have seen him, he was so handsome in his white-duck uniform. It is no wonder the lasses staying near their academy were always present in the school grounds when they did their parade in full uniform. In one of those days, Kuya was introduced to a beautiful lady who, without his knowledge, had been frequenting those parades because of him. She was barely sixteen years old and in love. Kuya was nineteen with one more year of schooling to graduate. They fell in love.

I would soon notice a change in Kuya. At night, when we would be at our usual hangout near the river, he would be silent for a long time. We used to fill these times with his stories of conquest, how he liked going to school in the academy, and about the girls that came to chat after classes were over. But lately, we just sat still. I asked a few times if something was wrong, he would look at me, shake his head, and not say anything. I sat with him until he was ready to go.

Many months later, Kuya would be at sea doing his internship; that absence fueled an intense desire for the lovers to forget themselves. Kuya had barely six months to go and an appointment to the Philippine Navy was waiting for him. But instead, one evening while we were having supper, Kuya came home with our soon-to-be *Ate*, who was pregnant.

The world of Tatay crumbled. He refused to come out of the room. Our *Tiang* Regina, who was living next door, came over and asked me to call Tatay. He was mad and didn't want to speak to anyone. He told me to tell Tiang Regina to convince Kuya to send Ate home. He would take care of all her needs, but please don't get married at that time.

His dream of having his firstborn follow his footsteps as an engineer was suddenly lost just like that. It was a promise he made to Apo Juli, that all his children would bring home diplomas and it was Kuya who was to be the pathfinder of this dream. But then, he got lost on the way. Not losing hope, he urged Kuya to finish his studies. But Kuya had good values he inherited from Tatay. He felt he must assume responsibility for his wife and school was no longer an option. He politely rejected Tatay's offer. And with sheer disappointment for his firstborn, he did not talk to Kuya for a long time.

This was the start of Kuya's trek on the rugged terrain of his life.

It took months before Kuya could find a job. Not having any savings, he had no choice but to keep his room in the house with our Ate, whose stomach grew bigger every day. His background as maritime engineer could not get him a job on land. Kuya no longer wanted to work in any seagoing vessel because his wife was about to deliver soon and he wanted to be there for her. He settled for a job as a maintenance man of a *paupahan*, work that saw him back to being a carpenter, mason, electrician, driver again. But this time, he was not paid in cash like what Tatay used to do for him. He was paid with food and a bed. Tatay was bitter and did not want to treat him anything but a hired hand, maybe even less. Those days, Kuya was made to work for food and sleep.

Because of Nanay's growing *tienda*, many people came to eat in her place. She had good PR and the head of the slaughterhouse liked the food she served. She often gave the man more than the usual serving and soon they were talking like friends. One day, the man saw Kuya deliver some soft drinks to the store and asked, *"Hindi ba anak mo 'yan?"*

Nanay said yes and explained Kuya's circumstances and Tatay's broken heart. That was why Kuya was being treated the way he was. The man had a good heart and offered Kuya a job as a driver. It was not much but may give him a start to live on his own.

They say, in any travel and this includes life itself, the most difficult to climb is the first hill. Kuya started his trek not knowing where his footsteps will bring him but the love for his wife and the coming baby kept him going. It was enough for him in the meantime. It was a sight to watch Kuya, driving a beaten down six by six army surplus truck. One time, he could be driving a truck full of cattle ready for slaughter, and then another time, you might see him hauling stones. He did anything they asked him. He drove his truck morning, noon, and night. He didn't mind because at last, he was trying to make it out on his own.

The coming of the first grandchild made things easier for Kuya. It was the one that softened Tatay's heart. Babies are always a blessing. The birth of our Lord in a manger was the one true announcement that God sent his son to recover his sinful children. The birth of Kuya's first child was the redeemer that Tatay was waiting for.

They were at that time living in one of the rooms for rent. He continued to do odd jobs for Tatay so he was now able to stay in the room for free. Baby Mary became the drops of water that rekindled the relationship between Tatay and his firstborn. Tatay learned to accept the reality that Kuya chose to stop schooling so he could take care of his family. Tatay then realized that he was made of the same stuff, too. Didn't he also assume responsibility for their family when his father died? This time it was Tatay who saw himself in Kuya and cradling Mary, he felt the proudest on this day.

Kuya's life was getting better slowly, one day at a time. He had more children and Tatay would come home from work early to play with his grandchildren. The hurt of the past was replaced with a father-and-son relationship envious to behold. Kuya at this time was already working with the giant food company, San Miguel. His engineering background was needed in the plant. Like Tatay, his deftness in working with machines became his route to further his career. By the time the company put up a branch in Cebu, Kuya was on top of the list to handle the beer brewing machineries. They put him on the fast track. He was supervisor by the time I myself was at the helm of Medichem, one of the companies of Unilab.

At least once a month when I would be in Cebu for work, I made it a point to visit Kuya and have something for his kids. Ate is a good cook and always, I would ask her to cook for me and my team. San Miguel loved Kuya so much that they allowed him to stay in one of their houses for free. And he more than paid for the free stay. His mind was working all the time and he came up with ways to use the waste product of their beer and he turned it into dry ice used for the transport of their ice cream products. In recognition of this feat, he was requested to come to Manila, and be among those given recognition as a top inventor of San Miguel. We were all there to share in his honor. Kuya came down the stage, searched for Tatay, and handed him the trophy. Tatay was floating on air, and, as Jesus was baptized by John in the river Jordan, the Holy Spirit, too, came that day, and Tatay said, "This is the son of whom I am so proud of."

Beer as a drink was a monopoly. Their management was able to persuade decision makers in government to declare it a crowded industry. But an enterprising Chinese businessman was able to find a way to convince then President Marcos to open the industry and erase its crowded status. This gave them competition.

In the beginning, the newcomer came in strong, forcing Kuya's company to retrench. It was their way of rebuilding their forces and regrouping before they could launch a strong counter attack. But in the meantime, cash flow was tight. The labor union opposed the move to cut manpower and negotiated for the company to go into *uno senotra* instead. The men were willing to get a pay cut by only working every other day. Kuya had to make a decision. The company was offering more than a generous early retirement pay so he took that opportunity.

But it was a miscalculation and it was too late.

The economy was also on a downtrend, even with his strong experience, there were no works available for him elsewhere. He was back to making both ends meet, working odd jobs again, anything that could help support his children. Sometimes, people took advantage of him, making him work more but paying him less. The money he got from his old company lasted for only as long as Ate could manage. Soon, it was all gone.

My parents were then already living in America. They said people can build their own dream in this land for as long as they are willing to work. It takes money and connection to get to America. My wife Sophia was well-attached to people in the foreign office and getting his documentation was a breeze. She put up the show money for Kuya to gain entry into the US. Soon he was on his way.

The economy during the time of the dictator was unbearable. We lost the prestige of being the fastest growing economy in Asia by the time Marcos was booted out of office. Filipinos, not being able to find jobs in the country, looked overseas. Ingenious Filipinos grabbed at every rope they could hold on to get jobs in countries many never even heard of. We produced new heroes, the Overseas Filipino Workers. They balanced the dwindling income of the country. Their remittances alone became the number one dollar generator that paid for our imports, especially oil. But there was hell to pay.

A new social phenomenon was born—loneliness. This psychologically affected the workers and those they left behind. It created emptiness too difficult to fill. Husbands and wives looked for other means to fill their loneliness. Families suffered, separation and annulment became rampant. The children suffered the most. They lost the love of parents who were forced to situations that economic conditions brought them to.

In the light of this phenomenon, Kuya, too, was a victim. They say men are polygamous by nature but this is not an excuse. And he did hold on as long as he could. Ate was his first love after all. But an uncanny situation became the conduit to losing his fidelity. America has funny laws. One is only able to work legally if you are married to a citizen. That was the only way.

In his desire to work legally, Kuya gave in, Ate filed for a divorce just for convenience. But the convenience became real. His new marriage may have worked to solve one of his problems but it created another.

For a while, he stayed with our parents. But since he chose companionship of someone the family did not know, he had to move out. Tatay and Nanay tried to understand his situation. Tatay welcomed Kuya and the new wife whenever they visited. The new girl wasn't so bad, it was just that for the family, Ate was the wife they knew only for Kuya. The girl was from a good family. She supported herself by working in a nursing home for the aged. The difficult times were those when the family celebrated occasions together. There was awkwardness with everyone thinking about Ate. And it was most uncomfortable for the children.

I have felt that discomfort myself one time when we came to celebrate Christmas in the US. We had traveled all the way from the Philippines to be with them. Kuya's new wife was there, his children and grandchildren from Ate. Naturally, there were exchanges of gifts. Mary's eldest approached to give her gift to Kuya. She kissed him to say hello, looked at the woman beside Kuya, and walked away. That kind of awkwardness tops my list. After the party, Mary wanted to speak with her father. She was adamant and wanted him to leave the woman out of respect for their mother. Kuya did not give any excuses, did not even give an explanation and just said, *"Paano naman ako?"*

At that moment, he lost the respect of his children.

But the Teacher understands. "My sympathies are with your brother, but still, it does not justify his actions, especially not in the eyes of God."

But Kuya's challenge did not end there. For one reason or another, his American dream never came to be. As much as jobs were available, they were all menial. Coupled with the Western standard of living, you barely make even when you take rent, food, and transport costs out. The promising jobs were reserved for those with titles attached to their names. Kuya then realized why Tatay insisted that he finish his studies. Opportunity seemed to come only to those who had a diploma to show for.

But Kuya carried on, unmindful of his difficulties. He had chosen a path in a lonely road so he ought to find his way from there. No opportunity was coming his way but the new wife was more optimistic than he was. Having acquired knowledge in running a placement agency for nurses, she convinced Kuya to bankroll the business she planned to put up. Where would Kuya get the money? There was no way for him to get a bank loan, he did not have anything for collateral. He had nowhere else to go but to return to Tatay and Nanay. They did not turn him away; they helped him as much as they could. But it wasn't enough. It was my wife, Sophia, who loaned them the balance.

At that moment, they were more hopeful of the future and tried to look for their own place under the sun.

Back home, Ate was her usual cheerful self. Bobby and Ronald, her two younger sons, lived with her. Her two older sons were already on their own, one in the US Navy and the other married and working as an aviation technician in Saudi Arabia. Her youngest daughter had already settled down on her own. When time permitted, Ate and my wife Sophia would meet and catch up on each other's lives. Sophia tried hard to keep a normal conversation, avoiding topics such as happenings in America. As careful as she was, Sophia sensed that Ate was already on to something. But she could not put her finger on it.

Like me, Ate is asthmatic, hers much worse than mine. Funny thing about asthmatics, we know when someone is having an attack or about to have one. Ate was fast moving into a worse condition. One of the reasons she used to come to our house regularly was to share my medications. Sophia and I made a very difficult decision at that time. So used to being neighbors with Ate, we decided to relocate somewhere in Quezon City nearer my workplace. So my asthmatic chats with Ate dwindled until it eventually stopped. Unknown to Sophia and I, the doctor had already placed Ate on adrenalin injection. She was advised to inject herself when she feels she can barely breathe anymore. And then, one day, her body stopped responding to adrenalin. Her hour had come.

In my personal thoughts, I prayed hard for God to spare me this experience. Even as I prayed, the smiling face of Ate was on my mind together with the sound of trumpets blowing as the angels slowly took her away.

Ate, on her deathbed, brought one more blessing to the family. Somehow her death helped the children look at Kuya with sympathy and forgiveness.

Back in the US, Kuya's business failed. Money was even harder to find in those days. He continued his struggle with his wife at his side. They heard that Las Vegas might have better opportunities. So he went and Kuya found a security job position in one of the casinos where his wife worked as a dealer. It was a pretty decent income for both of them but nothing to boast about. At least, it gave them some breathing space but not total financial independence.

And then it had to happen.

He was driving his run-down Toyota on his way to work when he felt a piercing pain. Kuya had the presence of mind to slow down and stop behind the curb. When he felt a little better, he drove himself to the nearest hospital. They gave him the necessary tests. The verdict: he needed a bypass. They put him on medication to ease his condition. And at that time he had this new hill to climb. "Should I still go on?" he asked himself.

He called his son Bobby who was closest to him. Bobby was a medic in the navy, maybe he can help. He had health insurance but it wasn't enough. So Kuya worried about the costs of the operation more than actually surviving it first.

This critical moment of Kuya's life is a blur to me. I don't know how his children responded to his needs. So I thought it best to capture the events with a narrative from Mary. Every son wants to have a good relationship with his father— what more a daughter. It is a natural desire to want to be daddy's little girl. For the lucky ones, this is not such a hard task. However, some are not as lucky. No one wants it to happen but many have strained and troubled relationships with their dads. And this affects the entire family. This leaves a hole in everyone's hearts.

Let us hear the thoughts of Kuya's eldest daughter:

The earliest memory I have of my Dad is one of me as a young girl holding his two fingers as we walked together. His hands were so large that I could only grip his two fingers. He always took me with him to my grandparents' house whenever he could get off from work. Although our visits were short, I could sense the excitement and anticipation of our arrival from the faces of my loving grandparents. I am the eldest grandchild, thus the "apple of their eye" as I lovingly joked around with my cousins. These visits made me feel closer to my grandparents, something that I will forever be grateful because it is a nurturing relationship that I will never forget.

As I got older, I remember Dad trying to give us the same attention in spite of longer hours at work. I remember Dad would walk my brother and I to school so our mom could stay home and take care of our younger sibling. I remember listening to his footsteps when he came home so that I could ask him for some money first before my other siblings could do. I would make a list of things and keep it in my pocket so I would be ready when he arrived. I being too small to go to the stores, my dad would schedule a shopping trip to the nearest store so that I could buy what I wanted. The jeepney ride was special because it afforded us to talk about school and about my other sister and brothers.

My father was a mechanic in the largest beer company in the Philippines. He worked long hours, sometimes even on weekends. I remember the times when my father would stop by the house during lunch break when we were already home from school. We would all camp out in the living room while he ate so we could be with him as we watched noontime television.

After lunch, dad would sit on his favorite chair, while we watched him fall into his nap. For a short period, we would watch him sleep peacefully while our mom busied herself with the household chores. After a short nap, he would bid us and our mom goodbye and off he went to work again. Life then was that simple and predictable. I loved every minute of it. When I was in sixth grade, my family left the home we've always known. My dad relocated to Cebu first. It was some sort of promotion with better pay and benefits. After about six months, the family joined him there. I stayed. They left me with my grandparents. But during Christmas break and summer vacation, I was in Cebu with them.

I remember my dad bringing me to his office and introduced his eldest daughter to his co-workers. These visits included a tour of the massive facility, from the preparation of bottles to beer making to packaging. He patiently explained how beer was made and what his actual work does for the company. I sensed pride in his eyes and his words. This pride became more apparent when he was awarded the "Innovator of the Year" for recycling waste materials from beer by-products into dry ice. This recognition was another feather in his cap. He worked for the company until he retired.

During retirement, my dad visited the USA where he would eventually immigrate to. It was also at this time that he and my mom divorced. My dad consequently remarried. The divorce placed a strain in our relationship. I started harboring resentment towards my dad because of the way things played out during their divorce.

In 1995, my dad had a heart attack which required an emergency open heart surgery. We all helped him. We set aside our differences, tried to forget our hurt feelings, and focused only on getting him back to his feet.

Working together with my brothers and sisters gave us all a chance to talk and to try to see the situation through our father's eyes. While we all believed that marrying another woman was wrong, especially since our mom was still alive, we were all willing to look past it. It was to be the start of our healing process.

I knew that if I didn't reconcile with my father, I would almost certainly regret it. Although the lines of communication had often been clogged between my dad and I, I knew it was never too late to rebuild our relationship. I was doing it for myself initially. But then it's more for him so that he could get his little girl back.

I realized what I have been missing in the last years that Dad and I didn't talk. Even my kids were cheated of a grandfather. When Dad was better and I finally found the time to talk to him, I was scared but knew that I had to get over it because all would be well soon. There was a new kind of love and acceptance that grew between us again. This time, I find it easy to talk to him again. My siblings are also always there for him now. We are a family again and fortunately, my dad is still here to enjoy it.

These are the thoughts of my niece and I find them truly refreshing. So although Kuya is on top of another hill in life, his children are now with him and I am sure they will be there as they walk down from it together.

CHAPTER XIII
The Seasons of Emmaus

Nanay and Tatay

Many of my age will have no difficulty relating to this story. The young, too, can learn from it. I am lucky to be in the family of my Tatay and Nanay. All of us are lucky because our parents loved us, even in their deathbed.

$\mathcal{T}$he persecution at the time of the Maccabees forced the Jewish ancestors to reflect on the fate of the martyrs and it became obvious that there would be no justice from God if he did not raise them to share a happy life with him. Since Hebrew culture did not make the distinction between body and soul, they said that people would emerge from dust, or they would have life begin on judgment day. And that on judgment day, we will all be welcomed because in its coming is also the arrival of our most awaited Savior.

At the same time, Greek culture influenced Israel: Greeks saw in each person something material, the body and soul (which gives life), and oftentimes different from the spirit, which is always in search of truth and good. For this reason, Wisdom, the last of the Old Testament books, says that the soul (or the spirit) is immortal and it meets God upon death. That is why we do not need to fear death, for death is a new beginning. *(Paraphrased from the Christian Community Bible)*

Cleopas reflects, "Life to me is like the seasons we go through year in and year out. Take, for instance, the weather here in Emmaus. Our typical weather here is like the season of life characterized by a Mediterranean climate. We have hot and dry summers mixed with cool and rainy winters. Light snow usually falls once or twice a year, although heavy snowfall can be expected every three to four years. January is the coldest month of the year; July and August are the hottest months. Temperatures vary widely from day to night and Emmaus evenings are typically cool even in the summer. I talk about the weather because I want you to understand how things were at the Master's crucifixion and how the seasons of Emmaus mimic life. We often speak of the mornings, noon, and evenings of our life in comparison with the seasons of the year. Thus dawn is the beginning of life, while noon exemplifies its robustness, and sunset is when we begin to reflect on what our life travels have brought us.

I understood clearly what Cleopas was trying to say. In fact, I shared thoughts with him that my family members, especially my wife, are luckier than most because we not only have a farm but a place where we can go to rest, to meditate, and to commune with nature. It is a retreat we can call our own, not needing to wait for the evening of our lives, so to speak.

God gifted us with a lovable, likable, and trustworthy group of people to help in the farm. Do you remember Juan, the man who assisted Sophia in building *Bahay Maria*? He has been our best find, a jewel we discovered living in the farm. He was popular and well-liked in our *barrio*. But sad to say, he passed away at such a young age. This is how I remember that day.

"Para akong nawalan ng dalawang paa, Uncle," was how Ka Mando described the loss everyone felt.

"Mabuti pang ako na ang namatay," Juan's widow cried endlessly.

It was an accident no one believed could have happened to Juan.

That morning was no different from any other day. Just like a typical morning in our farm, the day was full of promise. It always began with everything bright and beautiful. God must have needed someone with Juan's expertise in heaven to have gotten him from us so suddenly.

"Papa, Papa, na-ground ako," were the last words that Juan heard. Without thinking of his own safety, he rushed to his wife, and hit the TV antenna with a piece of wood. No one remembers what happened next. What everyone surmised was that he must have slipped and hit the antenna. He fell and his legs got caught in the TV post. The water on the embankment where he fell served like a conductor. The current surged and his body absorbed the full force of the shock. Juan saved his wife and didn't think he needed to save himself. Yet it was heroism that she didn't want in the first place. How she wished it was the other way around.

I met Juan when he was still a gangling youth. We just moved in the farm. Ka Mando, our *katiwala,* had a beautiful daughter named Juana. Like magnet, her charm caught Juan and he never let her go. And as tradition in our *barrio* dictates, a man seeking the hands of a woman serves her family to prove his sincere intentions. And Juan, always a gentleman, was a big help in the farm. Even when they were already married, he continued to be the handyman that put order in the things we needed *Ka Mando* to take care of. Juan did not expect anything from us. He was grateful for our presence. And in a way, we gave them hope, I remember Juan telling me months before. My wife who was always protective of the children in the farm made sure they had proper schooling. She wanted all of them to have better lives.

Juan was the project manager of the chapel we built in the farm. Sophia trusted him. She felt his presence that fatal morning while she was in the garden at home. Sometime between ten and eleven in the morning, she came to me and said, "Dad, I don't feel well. Is it alright if I will just follow later?" We were on our way out to a resort in Antipolo.

I left without her. While I was in the hotel room preparing for a round of golf, she called me crying, *"Dad, patay na si Juan."*

"Huh? What happened?" I replied in disbelief.

"Nakuryente daw," she said in between sobs. "I want Juan to stay in the chapel, *siya naman ang gumawa nuon, pwede ba, Dad?"*

"Of course," I said. I was worried about Sophia. She's been complaining of some shortness of breath, her blood sugar was up and the doctor wanted her to lose some weight to prevent any other complications. "Take it easy, Ma. Just pray for Juan. I am sure you will find a way to help the children later."

"Why do people so young, so good, and so full of promise die?" she asked.

"Only the good die young," I whispered.

"Why?" she persisted, "shouldn't God be taking away the rejects of society? *Wala naman silang pakinabang eh, di sila na lang ang kunin ng Diyos.*"

I was silent. I didn't know what to say. I had to convince myself of it, too. But I knew that God always had a reason. And that it is not for us to question God. We can only accept his grace in humility.

"Humility is grounded in the truth, in reality. It is based on the certitude that creature and Creator are separated by an infinite distance. Once it recognizes how God crosses that gulf for the sake of his beloved creatures, the soul grows in humility and gratitude" (*In Conversation with God*).

In his own way, Juan was as humble as one can be. "*Mayroon akong problema, Juan,*" Ka Mando would tell him during those times when everything seemed to go wrong. And Juan's quick reply was always, "*Wala kang problema, Tatay. Aayusin natin 'yan.*"

In his own little way, Juan assures his father-in-law that God has a way of taking care of things. That it is always for the best and that God will never bring them harm. Even when he was working in the company where I was once President, Juan always had a calming presence. When I would hear of some grumbling among the rank and file, I would tell him, "*Mukhang may problema tayo sa mga tao, Juan.*"

"Relax *ka lang, Boss, aayusin natin 'yan*," was always his mantra. And I believed every word he said.

That is the Juan that I knew, quick to help, trustworthy, *mahal ng mga tao*.

Juan is not gone. He will never be. We still feel his presence with Juana, with Josh and Ambrose, his children. He will be with *Ka Mando* and *Aling Lupe*, and with everyone that he loves. He will be in our chapel. He will be in the farm. In everything that surrounds us.

Still, I wanted us to bid him goodbye before he meets with the Creator and he shall speak of him to everyone in heaven and say, "This is my son of whom I am well pleased."

"*Paalam, Juan.*"

It was also one of those days in Emmaus. As usual, we waited for what the Teacher had to say. He interpreted the meaning of death with the story of *Gurion*, the kite.

It was the perfect day for kites to fly, a sky almost cloudless except for the occasional puff that blew a steady stream of easterly breeze towards the bay. Among the colorful kites flying that day, Gurion was aloft the highest. This was to be expected. In the hierarchy of kites, the Gurion, for which he was named after, lords over the makeshift *boca-boca*, mostly a piece of ruled writing paper properly folded to catch the breeze and flown by a hopeful school boy with a length of string "borrowed" from *Nanay's* sewing kit. Then there is the fairly decent type, the *tsapi-tsapi*, made of two pieces of thin bamboo skeleton tied together to form a cross on which *papel de japon* is glued. Next comes the handsome and complex Golondrina. Perhaps due to its shape reminiscent of the bottle of popular soda, it looks a bit feminine. But there is no denying the hours of meticulous labor that went to its fabrication. In flight, the Golondrina is as graceful as a butterfly.

But it all pales in comparison to the mighty Gurion. In Malabon many years ago, competitions were held to determine the biggest and the highest flying Gurions. Some models were reported to be bigger than eight feet tall! It required an inch thick abaca twine and at least two able-bodied kite flyers to keep it aloft. From the Gurion's vantage height, he could look down rather vainly at the lesser co-flyers. He is able to remain almost immobile against a stiff air current. He would sway left and right and sidewise or execute a sharp dive then recover his former altitude at the bidding of his flyer. He was tethered with a thick cotton twine. The other kites could only look up and admire Gurion.

But Gurion was restless. He envied the pigeons that freely flew in perfect formation. At his height, there were the more daring *maya* birds that seemed to taunt him with their free flight. The roar of a passing jetliner would further whet the appetite of Gurion for more altitude. And above anything else, he craved for the freedom of an unfettered flight! He imagined how wonderful it must be if his owner were to let go of the cotton twine. He will be free to fly with the birds. He can go to places other than the familiar and monotonous seaside terrain.

Gurion was in this frequent wishful state when there was a sudden gust of inordinately strong wind. The pull was too much for the cotton twine. Gurion felt the sudden release of his owner's grasp. The cotton twine snapped and sent him on a free flight. At last, Gurion was free! He danced merrily as he floated with the breeze. A slight updraft carried him even higher. Then a moderate easterly wind blew him towards the sea. Fantastic, he can only exclaim as he was carried even farther until he could no longer see the shores. Then the winds died down. Sailors are all too familiar with this phenomenon called doldrums! It was very much feared by the mariners of the sailboat days. Gurion was caught by surprise. Instead of staying aloft, he was then starting to lose altitude and drop straight down the sea! Panic! The sea will certainly dissolve his delicate *papel de japon*.

During his plunge downwards, he had time to realize the real value of his owners' controlling pulls and tags! How he misses the cotton twine which kept him securely anchored in his owner's hands. It was his umbilical cord. A kite like him needed the opposing forces of the push of the winds and the pull of the cotton twine held by his flyer. Kites can only fly against the seemingly adversarial force of the wind. Gurion continued spiraling downward.

Then… splash!

And so it is also with our daily existence.

Why does God allow suffering and sorrows? Generations before us had repeatedly asked this question. Why do innocent God-fearing people suffer? A contemporary author stated it as—*Why do bad things happen to good people?* Why are babies born with epilepsy? or Down's syndrome? or even totally blind? Why do young people with a lot of promise die? Why are there wars with a magnitude of innocent civilians as casualties?

There has been no easy and readily acceptable answer to this age-old profound question.

It has always been convenient to blame God. Wasn't he supposed to control all the workings in the universe? Some of us feel aggrieved that we raise our fist, tightly clenched, towards heaven for an undeserved punishment from the heavy hand of the Creator. Some regular churchgoers feel betrayed. But most tragic of all, a few turn their backs completely and declare—"There is no God!"

We must always remind ourselves that when God made man, he made him perfect. He not only promised him a rose garden, he gave him the Garden of Eden. He even gave him a mate. Man and woman lived in utopia. However, God had one condition. Just like Gurion, our couple-ancestors craved for loftier heights. They rebelled against the Creator, fully realizing the consequences of their crime in exchange for the benefits the serpent promised them. As soon as they cut the sacred cord that tied them with God, they tumbled down. *Therefore, just as through one person sin entered the world, and through sin, death, and thus death came to all, inasmuch as all sinned* (Romans 5:12). The decision to rebel was solely theirs. The responsibility was theirs. Not God's.

Similarly, most of the troubles we encounter in our life we bring on ourselves through our thoughtlessness and carelessness. For example, we trip and fall down the stairs because we are too lazy to switch on the light to guide us. Or we risk driving along a one-way street and find ourselves colliding with an oncoming vehicle. Indeed, most of the accidents we encounter could have been totally avoided if only we were careful. If only we listened. And if only we believed that the rules were meant to protect us.

Those who have lost a loved one through death are expectedly inconsolable, even if the lost one is now freed of the extreme pain and discomfort of a dreadful illness. Again God is blamed, the Creator of the creature now fully reposed. It is a form of selfishness to wish for the continued company of a seriously afflicted loved one who himself could very possibly prefer the end to his suffering. God intends for that sorrow to affect something profound for the bereaved. Much later, he will thank God because he has become a better person than he would have been without that sorrow.

Someone wrote that with all the sorrows, disappointments, and frustrations, God is opening up a path for the afflicted. One cannot turn away from that path without losing his reason for it being opened.

Dr. Leslie D. Weatherhead, Minister-Emeritus, President of the Institute of Religion and Medicine, London, wrote:

> "We must at the outset give up the idea that the providential care of God is limited to his activity in giving us the things we call good, like health, success, freedom from physical frustration in terms of food, power and sex; the things we

lump together and call 'all the blessings of this life.' His providence is rather in providing for possibilities of reaction with which we must, with all the power and insight which his grace affords, proceed to build character and develop insight, remembering that his aims can be reached just as surely by a right use of things we call evil—like bereavement, pain, suffering, sorrow, frustration, and so on—as by a right use of the things we call good."

Clearly God permits problems and crises to enter our lives so that he can all the more bring his love alive in our experience.

God proclaimed: *"I have told you this so that you might have peace in me. In the world you will have trouble, but take courage, I have conquered the world"* (John 16:33).

Saint Paul followed this up with his affirmation: *"We know that all things work for good for those who love God, who are called according to his purpose"* (Romans 8:28).

Again from Dr. Leslie Weatherhead: "...we may liken life to a journey, the end of which we cannot see, and we have to learn how to be good travelers, and learn how to cope with the hills and the mists, using all the aids offered, and especially the companionship of the One who promised to travel with us."

I did not want to speak anymore but the Teacher insisted that I share my thoughts. So I said:

Earlier, Cleopas spoke of the seasons of Emmaus and how they mimic life. Let me add sunset—a time we look forward to as an opportunity to rest. It is when the sun begins to go down; the coolness of the evening caresses the warmth of the afternoon which prepares us to call it a day. I am in the sunset of my life. Seven decades and one year ago, that's how much I've spent in this wonderful world full of expectations. Now here I am waiting for the final call.

And so I found myself sitting by the beach. The span of sand running the shore runs for miles. From end to end, my calculations were that it would take one about an hour to jog through the landscape. It was high tide. Should you want to go further, you could have the freedom of a dive and meet the roaring waves.

I sat motionless. The travel brochure was right. It would take a lifetime to engulf the beauty of this beach in Clearwater, Tampa, Florida. I started watching the sunset as its colors changed like a chameleon adapting to the drifting clouds hanging like curtains on a sill. Very much like a rainbow after a short downpour when the sunbursts meet the retreating rain. It's a beauty difficult to describe. I'd dare say it is a panorama at the tip of the poet's ink. There I was in deep concentration as the colors slowly turned from bright yellow to crimson red.

I have seen this same sunset many times along Manila Bay. Yet, there was something about this sunset in Clearwater Bay. The sun did not go below the horizon. It seemed to stop inches before it touched the line and disappeared in the clouds. It seemed to say, "No, I don't want to fall, I'll just hide behind the clouds." The light also remained. It took some time before darkness was upon me.

I watched this sunset as I watched life around me.

This time I was sitting in a restaurant with my wife and my younger son. There was a couple eating silently in the corner. I felt only sadness for them. I tugged at my wife, "Ma, look at the old couple in the corner. They're not talking anymore. They seem so lost in their own thoughts."

"No, Dad, maybe they're just tired," she said putting brightness in her voice. "Don't worry, you and I will always have something to talk about. Our years are full of memories waiting for us to reminisce and reflect upon them."

"Okay, I believe you," I said holding her hand tightly.

And I remember another sunset of life.

"*Sino ka?*" she asked.

"*Inay, si David 'yan, anak mo sa Manila,*" my older sister replied.

"*Ako ito, Inay, kilala mo ako?*"

"*Hindi ba asawa ka ni Pietro?*"

She heard laughter all around. I wonder if she understood what the laughter meant. The woman asking her was my wife and Pietro is my younger brother. *Nanay* can no longer put names on faces. Our only hope is that in the sunset of her years, she will still have the quality of life we can only pray for.

Our *Inay* did not have the mind that built civilization. She is not a Socrates or a Plato who put forth philosophies that continue to rule our lives. Neither was she a genius like Newton or Einstein. She wasn't even close to being a Shakespeare who defined what art is. Yet, in the end, they are what they are—mortals. Just like my *Inay*.

Time has a way of leveling the playing field. Rich or poor, bright or dumb, the mind has a way of knowing when to stop. I saw this in the life of the most powerful person I've worked with personally. His was the brain of a genius. Nothing he put his mind into got lost. He was so wealthy; he didn't need to know how much he had. He once told me, "David, when you are still able to count your money, you have a long way to go before you can call yourself rich." Then time and age caught him and brought him into a web of forgetfulness. His money served him little. The last time we shook hands and bid farewell, he could hardly recognize me. He just smiled blankly. It was the saddest smile I have ever seen on anyone.

Many are lucky to leave the world with their minds intact—to remember how nice it is to be young and to feel the boundless energy we once had. But to those who experience the sunset of life not knowing where it begins or ends, we can only wish that the blessedness of forgetfulness will grant them a serene ending when it matters.

My teacher Khalil Gibran has these wise words about time:

"This world is but a winery, its host and master is father time, which caters only to those steeped in dreams of discordant, without rhyme. For people drink and race as though they were the steeds of mad desire; thus some are blatant when they pray, others frenzied to acquire.

"The people of the city abuse the time of wine, for they think upon it as a temple, and they drink of it with ease and with unthinking, and they flee, scurrying into old age with deep but unknowing sorrow."

So, when we begin to move on, to struggle, and to pay homage to the one God who loves us, we will all have no claim to our richness or greatness here on earth. In the life that I have led, I pray that in its ordinariness, God will find fullness in my life. When my time comes, I want to hold on to his hand knowing he will take me with him. And I will whisper to him with utmost gratitude, "Thank you for the life journey."

And when death is upon me, I will welcome it because I know I have had a good life. And the man on the road to Emmaus is waiting for me with open arms. He will get himself ready for me. And I will run into him, feeling that this is where I belong now.

This makes me remember my *Tatay*.

I have not seen a man so much in love with life like my Tatay was. He was a loving husband to my Nanay, who was equally in love with life. As a boy, he absorbed life for what it was, even with the unending struggles. He picked himself from the ashes of poverty, set his sights on higher grounds and got ready to face whatever the world would bring. His lack of formal education became the motivation to learn more. He read anything that caught his eyes and always looked ahead for what the future held for him.

His break finally came when the country needed professionals to replace the depleted ranks of engineers, accountants, doctors, and scientists because of the big war. He took the test for the professional licensed engineer and aced it. It was to be the most important stepping stone to his dream. He could easily have rested on his laurels when he retired but that wasn't Tatay. He moved on to a new career after retirement.

As his waking days were spent loving life, his children, too, went out to master life's challenges. His mornings ushered days of beginnings, days that painted beauty in the garden of life, where the search for wisdom were planted with flowers, bushes, and trees and where fireflies flew. Tatay hated going to sleep. He would rather watch the stars and the moon, and witness the brilliance that poets romanticize.

On many occasions, Tatay would tell us his stories of conquest. Stories that spoke of life's complexities—the lessons of love, the adventures of bravery, and the permanent marks left in our hearts and minds.

Tatay heard what Dr. Andrew Lance of Bethsaida Medical Center said, "You have cancer. I do not know how much time you have. It is best that I check you in the hospital for more tests."

Tatay didn't feel like dying. Except for the lump in his throat, he felt great. An arm wrestling match with the doctor anytime would settle this argument. Besides, he was just eighty years young and strong as a bull. So Tatay picked up the phone and called Sarah. She's an oncologist and she was his daughter. So she would know better.

Nanay was calm. She said that the news devastated Tatay, "Why now, why cancer?" He told Nanay, "No, I won't accept that. You will see. When Sarah arrives, she will tell me Dr. Lance is wrong. I'm strong as a bull."

He could not believe that his years of struggle for a better life were coming to end. Moving to America did not come easy. It was a struggle, a never-ending climb against biases that came in all forms. Discrimination against migrants was thick. The battle for acceptance had to be overcome, one step at a time. But Tatay never looked back. He plodded his way through every difficulty. He was dead set on making it in America.

Then here comes the doctor telling him that he will die soon? Nonsense!

But we knew what was happening. It was just Tatay refusing to accept the news. Nanay cried whenever she heard Tatay cough continuously through the night, struggling for breath. No medicine could ease his pain. We all prayed for a miracle. But Nanay wasn't saying much at that time.

Ate Anna, my sister staying in Manila, was packing in haste. The cry for help, the helplessness in Nanay's voice was a warning that things may turn from bad to worse. She feared for Nanay, knowing how close she is to Tatay.

"Anna," *Nanay* pleaded, "Come quickly, I need help, I can't do this alone. *Baka mahalata ng Tatay mo na nagluluksa ako!*" (Your *Tatay* may think I am already mourning!)

"*Lakasan mo ang loob mo, 'Nay, baka mauna ka pa kay Tatay,* be strong," Ate Anna reminded her again and again. *Kuya* Rene, her husband, understood why she had to go. Even her children wished her well. She would keep in touch with them while in America. But right now, she had to be with her parents.

Ate Anna was like a second mother to all of us. And with her being with us gave everyone some sense of peace. She met with Sarah in New York and together, they read the report of Dr. Lance. The reality of his findings was exact. It was thorough and there was no room for Sarah to maneuver. It took her hours looking for a loophole but in the end, Dr. Lance was correct. There was nothing wrong with his finding although she really wished there was.

Plans then had to be made before time caught up with Tatay. His deterioration would be fast. We ought to find a way to ease his pain and give Tatay as much quality of life during his final days. We all came into agreement on how we will take care of Tatay's final days. My siblings wanted me to take charge. While this was all going on, the doctors watched Tatay in amazement. They said the infection has spread and he may have barely two months. But he has fought hard and we were all still hoping he would win. But Tatay already knew he was losing. And as intensely as he fought, every inch and every square of his body was then being invaded by the disease. It was not giving up, too.

Every waking hour, Tatay would look at our faces, remembering and etching in his memory every contour, every angle of his children. He wished to bring these mental pictures with him as he would say his final goodbye.

Then he asked, "Where is David?"

I was not there.

On the phone, Nanay was sobbing but trying to hold back. "David, don't wait anymore."

Tatay was fighting the pain, resisting the hands of his guardian angel. Tatay waited, in vain. Because when Nanay finally said, "David is on his way. He said you don't have to wait for him," Tatay let go. He passed away peacefully.

Tatay was a lucky man. He passed away with memories of his life intact. He was assured that the values he grew up with would live with his children. Even the doctors were surprised to see him live that long, they said it was us who kept him going. Tatay knew that during the most critical part of his life, we had set aside our petty misunderstandings and hurts so that we could be with Tatay in his last moments in peace.

The cancer caused Tatay to be angry with God, he felt very much betrayed. He questioned God for his suffering and in his pain, he waited for an answer. But God was not listening.

No answer came. It was I who helped him accept his fate. The distance between us helped in looking for a way for him to see the way of the Lord.

With my recorder, I sent him my prayers. I prayed like a child; I asked for God's guidance the way I used to when I was a little boy. That was when Tatay realized why the Lord was calling for him at that time. I prayed, "Lord, please help Tatay. He loves you with the same kind of love he gave us, maybe even more. We are what we are, and in his goodness and faith, he made sure we feared you. More than fear, he taught us to love you freely, with the passion only our childhood's faith can bring. He gave us the path for a life of comfort; we will not suffer from want. Now, Lord, my Tatay is again preparing our way to you. We need him, Lord, to be with you, to speak in our behalf. And we know Lord, that with Tatay at your side, he will continue to guide us and protect us from all occasions of sin."

I believe this prayer made Tatay accept God's wisdom. It is time, he probably thought. God needed him then for his own children's sake.

As I look back at the experience of Tatay's passing, I am in deep appreciation of the strength Nanay showed in the saddest moment of our lives. She held us together. When some of my sisters were ready to break down, she was the dam that prevented the water from rushing into the ocean of grief. My mother was an island of calm. The guests that came in the wake to offer their condolences were in awe of the peace she possessed. It was Nanay who soothed the frayed nerves of our relatives and friends. She was offering them words of joy in her hour of bereavement.

But in the final moment when Tatay was being laid to rest, Nanay's impregnable wall of calm broke. I held on to her tightly because I wanted to help ease the heaviness of her grief. It was a moment none of us anticipated. Nanay finally realized that Tatay was gone for good. And for the first time in her life, she felt alone. She would miss Tatay very much; life would never be the same again. Even Nanay was never going to be the same again.

In life and in death, I have never seen a couple so in love like my Tatay and Nanay was. On his deathbed, he promised Nanay that he would constantly watch heaven's window for her coming. He wanted to make sure that when Nanay arrived, he would be there to take her to the beautiful places in heaven. He felt a little guilty for saying that but Tatay also knew that life after his death would never be the same again. And there was no way to convince Nanay or himself otherwise.

But Tatay kept his. It really did feel like he was waiting for her. Everyone said so, especially my sister Nina who took care of Nanay in the last years of her life. She said that somehow, she knew Tatay was waiting because when it was time to go, she just smiled and went to sleep. There was none of the heaving for the last breath that her nurse warned them about. She just went with a smile. It was the signal Tatay was waiting for. Ever so gently, he probably took Nanay's hand and allowed the guardian angels to gently whisk her to him.

Nanay has left us as well but her smell lingered. We would have those memories of her to live by. Tatay waited for her for twenty years. It was now his turn to be with her.

Of course, we all felt the pain of Nanay's passing. We especially felt that pain in the sound of Kevin crying, one of Nanay's great-grandchildren. The sound of his grief pierced through our hearts. He was pleading for his *Lola* not to go. Nina took him in her arms. And as Nanay's casket was slowly being pushed to her final resting place, she asked him to look, "Look Kevin, your Lola will just lie right beside your Lolo. Now they will be together. Your Lolo has been waiting for her."

Kevin smiled. It was the same smile on Nanay's face when she took her last breath. It was the signal that Tatay left for Nanay. It was the same signal that Kevin saw. In his mind, he knew Lolo and Lola would then be together forever.

All her children loved her in their own special way. Mine was sort of a long-distance love. Being the only one who made the choice to make a living in our own country, I did not have the pleasure of being physically in touch with her, though I love her no less.

Like my father before her, I missed the chance of seeing her alive before she went away. But this time, my brothers and sisters made her passing less painful for me. In her final moments when they were all together praying and singing her favorite church songs, they let me be part of the experience. No matter how little it was, I had the joy of hearing her mumble a reply when I told her I love her.

"I love you, *Nanay*. I know you want to go. *Tatay* is waiting. *Huwag mo na akong hintayin, Inay. Lumakad ka na. Ikumusta mo ako kay Tatay.*"

My voice broke in grief. Why do people have to die? I thought to myself.

"Let me answer that for you, David," the Teacher interrupted my thoughts.

The mystery of life remains. Many times we are unable to explain the things happening around us. We challenge our intellect to understand the ways of the Lord, but no matter how much we try, we will never be able to fully comprehend God's wisdom.

Father Simplicio R. Apalisok, Jr. in his book, *Markings in the Desert*, attempted to offer some explanations:

> "Christ gives us the solution to the riddle: lose life so that God can come in. We need to deny our self-will and self-regard to be able to say to God, 'Thy will be done.' We are led to the pivotal and engaging desire: love of God. Only when we consecrate our life to him… to die ourselves… will he grant us the gift of true life."

As Teilhard de Chardin explains in *The Divine Milieu*:

> "We can set no limits to the tearing up of the roots that is involved in our journey to God… what will be the agent of that definitive transformation? Nothing less than death… God must, in one way or another, make room for

him, following us out and emptying us, if he is to finally penetrate into us."

My heart continues to bleed for the loss of my parents. But in my sadness, it has also led me to find joy. I have learned to rejoice in their death, for it is only through it that they found each other surrounded by the peace of the Lord. Their death was a blessing because it was in their passing that they also left us peace. The values I learned from Tatay and Nanay, like the star of Bethlehem, will lighten my own way to Jesus soon when my time will come.

CHAPTER XIV

Breaking of the Bread in Emmaus

$\mathcal{W}$e could almost see the town of Emmaus from where we were standing. Our journey had been a long one and it was finally ending. Our walk was almost over, night was fast approaching and it was time for a meal. We stopped before an inn and took our seats around a table. There were not that many people.

While waiting for the food, the Teacher looked at me and said, "David, tell me one more."

I decided to tell him about a piece I wrote called "Disturbing." It was about the movie *The Passion of The Christ*. Towards the end of the film was a drop of water. And that drop of water said it all.

New life is born. And from his pit, Satan howled. He knew Jesus was here to stay. The Passion of Christ was meant to give birth to new life. Our deliverance came through amazing miracles. Adam and Eve lost paradise in the Garden of Eden. God gave us a chance to recover the Garden with Noah spearheading the drive for salvation. God "washed" the earth for forty days and forty nights. When he finally stopped the deluge, the sun came out. A dove carried the leap that ushered a new beginning for mankind. But still, man wasted that.

The forty years of travel in the desert was marked with constant disobedience. The golden calf was the symbol of that dishonor. Moses lost the chance to enter Canaan because of this. And when we were already in the Promised Land, we followed the dictum of the Law but still not its substance. So we prayed in the temple and cursed even before our backs are turned from the tabernacle. Still God persisted. Instead of punishing us which we rightly deserve, he sent his Son to save us. Then he died for us. He was like a lamb thrown into the den of wolves. With his death, Satan thought he won. Evil now dominate the good. But Satan got it wrong. That one drop of water representing the blood of Christ was our new hope.

My wife captured in one word the effect the movie had on her; "disturbing" was what she said. *The Passion of The Christ* was truly unsettling and unnerving.

A Filipino friend said, "It's a miracle movie." An American friend saw it from another perspective. He did not find anything significant about the movie. "I was disappointed," he said. "After all those big brouhaha the big media build up, they ended with nothing." It was true; he saw nothing but horror and gore.

But the story of *The Passion of The Christ* was not meant to entertain. If anything, the movie wanted to remind people that the predictions in the Book of Revelation are now more accurate than ever. Man is going back to his old ways, openly defying and challenging God's ways. Of course, there will be hell to pay.

I now know why the Catholic Bishops' Conference asked people to watch it with open minds and not hate the Jews afterwards. Mark, one of the apostles, says it best in his Gospel (15:6-15).

Now on the occasion of the feast [Pilate] used to release to them one prisoner whom they requested. A man called Barabbas was then in prison along with the rebels who had committed murder in a rebellion. The crowd came forward and began to ask [Pilate] to do for them as he was accustomed. Pilate answered, "Do you want me to release to you the king of the Jews?" For he knew that it was out of envy that the chief priests had handed him over.

But the chief priests stirred up the crowd to have him release Barabbas for them instead. Pilate again said to them in reply, "Then what [do you want] me to do [with the man you call] the king of the Jews?"

They shouted again. "Crucify him."

Pilate said to them, "Why? What evil has he done?"

They only shouted the louder, "Crucify him."

So Pilate, wishing to satisfy the crowd, released Barabbas to them and, after he had Jesus scourged handed him over to be crucified.

And the Jews, the chosen people, sealed their fate forever.

One cannot help but pity the Jews. Their misery, their disappointment for their existing condition, their ignorance, and their envy inflamed hatred for a Man that did them no wrong. Christ's death was the beginning of the decline of a nation so loved by God. He gave them the land of promise, but for what? The people that God loved so much, the people with whom he made a covenant to love and protect, crucified his beloved Son. It is no wonder that generations after generations of Jews continue to roam the earth with no place to call their own.

So much was written about their holocaust. But the holocaust was in fact a glorious day, a victory. Finally, the sympathy of nations recovering from the devastation of a big war granted them the one thing they can never have, a piece of land. And yet, their find created another upheaval that today continue to sow fear and hatred among the Jews and the Islamic world. Maybe it is God's way of cleansing them. What do you think?

It is an unusual movie, this *The Passion of The Christ*. People left the theater silent. In deep thought, engrossed within. There was this feeling of guilt that for every pounding of the nail, each stroke was made heavier by the brunt of our sins. After all the years of praying the Rosary, especially the Sorrowful Mysteries, it took this movie for me to truly understand what the passion really means and why Jesus died for me. He said, "I am the way, the truth, and the light. No one comes to the Father except through me." Now I get it. I really do.

The movie made me understand the real pains that Jesus went through. I now know that every slash of the whip, every drop of blood, every wound indicted by the Romans was a stroke of every sin that I have committed. And yet Jesus rose above it all, "Forgive them, they did not know, they did not know."

It is a lesson of understanding and of humility. It is to know what it means to be a Catholic and, as a believer, to really understand that what God did as man was the only way he could bring me back to the side of his Father, that without his suffering I would have never had the chance to be free of my sins and the clutches of evil. The Book of Wisdom, 18:14-16; 19:6-9, captured in essence the message of the movie:

For when peaceful stillness compassed everything
and the night in its swift course was half spent,
Your all-powerful word from heaven's royal throne
bounded, a fierce warrior, into the doomed land,
bearing the sharp sword of your inexorable decree.
And as he alighted, he filled every place with death;
he still reached to heaven,
while he stood upon the earth.

For all creation, in its several kinds,
was being made over anew,
serving its natural laws,
that your children might be preserved unharmed.
The cloud overshadowed their camp;
and out of what had before been water,
dry land was seen emerging:
Out of the Red Sea an unimpeded road,
and a grassy plain out of the mighty flood.
Over this crossed the whole nation sheltered
by your hand,
after they beheld stupendous wonders.
For they ranged about like horses,
and bounded about like lambs,
praising you, O Lord! their deliverer.

I told my wife the same thing I felt about the movie, "disturbing."

The death of the Master must have more meaning for us to see. It must be like a seed planted on fertile soil, watered regularly, fertilized so it will grow to help people understand that they now have a chance to redeem themselves from total damnation. This man who died gave us the way to pave through the path of goodness that leads to the Father. He forgave. This is the lesson he is leaving us to learn—to forgive. When Peter asked the Master how many times he must forgive people, he replied, "seventy times seven times." It means endless.

We should not be discouraged when sometimes the Lord does not seem to hear us. There is a beautiful lesson hidden somewhere in his words when he asks you to listen to him. The noise of anxiety and the sound of anticipating problems before they even come deaden our hearing. We think God should be at our beck and call, expecting to answer our pleadings when we want it. But believe that God is listening, always. Yet we must also understand that the Lord distinguishes what is right for us and he will give us our desires in his own good time. In our prayers let us consider that we are God's best friend who knows what is good for us. "This is my beloved son, listen to him." God speaks to us in our prayer to seek the intercession of his son. And remember all the saints in heaven are loved by God but most of all, he loves the Mother of his Son and when you think everything is lost, that God continues not to listen, the Blessed Mother can show us how to go about it. Do you recall what she said in the miracle at Cana?

"Do whatever he tells you," she advises us.

Her son has a soft heart for the Mother; he will surely listen to her pleading. "These words of the Virgin Mary are a permanent invitation to carry out the resolutions that God our Lord suggest to us each day in our personal prayers" (Saint Jose Maria Escriva). So take these words to heart, "This is my beloved son, listen to him."

It was time for the meal. And what I heard was no ordinary grace before meals that the Lord had offered that evening in Emmaus. *And it happened that, while he was with them at table, he took bread, said the blessing, broke it, and gave it to them. With that their eyes were opened and they recognized him, but he vanished from their sight. Then they said to each other, "Were not our hearts burning [within us] while he spoke to us on the way and opened the scriptures to us?"* (Lk 24:30-32).

I felt my shoulder shaking, my wife was calling my name, "Dad, Dad, wake up you're dreaming." I woke up extremely tired. As I brushed away the heaviness of my eyes, I heard the haunting melody of the music that completed the message of my dream:

You Raise Me Up

When I am down and, oh my soul, so weary;
When troubles come and my heart burdened be;
Then, I am still and wait here in the silence,
Until you come and sit awhile with me.

You raise me up, so I can stand on mountains;
You raise me up, to walk on stormy seas;
I am strong, when I am on your shoulders;
You raise me up to more than I can be.

I looked beside me and Sophia was still asleep. Where was the song coming from? It didn't matter. Because my heart is full and I have come a long way from home called Emmaus.

THE WAY

Thus says the Lord, the Holy One of Israel:

O people of Zion, who dwell in Jerusalem,
no more will you weep;
He will be gracious to you when you cry out,
as soon as he hears he will answer you.
The Lord will give you the bread you need
and the water for which you thirst.
No longer will your Teacher hide himself,
but with your own eyes you shall see your Teacher,
While from behind, a voice shall sound in your ears:
"This is the way; walk in it,"
when you would turn to the right or to the left.
He will give rain for the seed
that you sow in the ground,
And the wheat that the soil produces
will be rich and abundant.
On that day your cattle will graze
in spacious meadows;

The oxen and the asses that till the ground
will eat silage tossed to them
with shovel and pitchfork.
Upon every high mountain and lofty hill
there will be streams of running water.
On the day of the great slaughter,
when the towers fall,
The light of the moon will be like that of the sun
and the light of the sun will be seven times greater
[like the light of seven days].
On the day the Lord binds up the wounds of his people,
he will heal the bruises left by his blows.

—Isaiah 30:19-21, 23-26

www.ingramcontent.com/pod-product-compliance
Lightning Source LLC
Chambersburg PA
CBHW030155070426
42447CB00031B/287